Java Projects for Beginners

Learn Java Programming by Building Real
Desktop Applications

By

STEM School

This Page Left Intentionally Blank

Contents

Chapter 1

Introduction to Java and Project-Based Learning

1.1 Why Java for Desktop Applications?

Java has been a cornerstone of application development since the mid-90s, and despite the rise of newer languages, its importance remains unshaken—especially in the realm of desktop applications. What makes Java unique is its "write once, run anywhere" philosophy. Java programs are compiled into platform-independent bytecode, which runs on the Java Virtual Machine (JVM). This means the same code can run on Windows, macOS, Linux, and even embedded systems without modification.

Java is backed by decades of development, libraries, frameworks, and a massive community. For desktop applications specifically, Java offers powerful tools such as **Swing**, **JavaFX**, and **AWT**, which enable developers to create robust graphical user interfaces (GUIs). While JavaFX is modern and rich in visual capabilities, Swing remains a reliable workhorse—lightweight, easy to grasp, and still widely used in enterprise systems.

Another benefit is Java's strong typing system, automatic memory management via garbage collection, and object-oriented nature. All of these features combine to help beginner developers write stable, maintainable, and efficient applications.

1.2 The Power of Project-Based Learning

There's a saying in engineering "Tell me, and I forget. Show me, and I remember. Involve me, and I understand." This captures the essence of project-based learning (PBL). Unlike passive learning, where students absorb facts without applying them, PBL emphasizes **active involvement**, allowing learners to construct knowledge through real-world tasks.

In our journey through this book, we won't just be reading about code—we'll be building things. Each chapter will introduce a mini-project. These projects are not arbitrary—they're designed to sharpen key skills in Java while reinforcing software development practices like modularity, error handling, event-driven programming, and user interface design.

The result is not only a stronger grasp of Java but also a valuable portfolio of applications that can demonstrate your capabilities to peers, clients, or employers.

1.3 Installing Java and Getting Set Up

Before we write a single line of Java code, let's get our development environment up and running. You'll need the **Java Development Kit (JDK)** and an **IDE**

(Integrated Development Environment) to write, debug, and run your code.

Step 1 Downloading and Installing the JDK

We'll be using the latest **Java SE (Standard Edition)** for this book. As of writing, **JDK 21** is the recommended LTS (Long Term Support) version.

Instructions

1. **Go to the official Oracle JDK page** https //www.oracle.com/java/technologies/javase-jdk21-downloads.html
2. **Choose your operating system** Select your platform (Windows, macOS, or Linux) and download the installer.
3. **Run the installer** Follow the on-screen instructions. By default, it will install Java to a directory like
   - Windows `C \Program Files\Java\jdk-21`
   - macOS `/Library/Java/JavaVirtualMachines/jdk-21.jdk`
   - Linux `/usr/lib/jvm/java-21`
4. **Verify the installation** Open a terminal or command prompt and run

   ```
   java -version
   ```

   You should see output similar to

   ```
   java version "21" 2023-09-19 LTS
   ```

Step 2 Setting Up the IDE

You can choose from multiple IDEs, but we recommend either **IntelliJ IDEA Community Edition** or **Eclipse IDE for Java Developers**.

Option A IntelliJ IDEA

1. Download from <u>https //www.jetbrains.com/idea/download</u>
2. Install and launch the application.
3. On the welcome screen, select **"New Project"** > **Java**.
4. Point to the installed JDK if not detected automatically.
5. Select "Create project from template" and choose "Command Line App".

Option B Eclipse

1. Download from https //www.eclipse.org/downloads
2. Choose **Eclipse IDE for Java Developers**.
3. After installation, launch Eclipse and select a workspace directory.
4. Go to **File > New > Java Project**.
5. Enter project name `HelloGUIProject`
6. Right-click the `src` folder > New > Class > Name it `Main`, check "public static void main(String[] args)".

Quick Comparison Table

Feature	IntelliJ IDEA	Eclipse
UI Design	Modern, intuitive	Feature-rich, customizable
Performance	Optimized, fast indexing	Lightweight, quicker startup
Community	Large, active JetBrains	Very active, open-source base
Best For	Beginners, modern devs	Eclipse plugin developers

1.4 Writing Your First GUI Program – "Hello, GUI!"

To test our setup and dip our toes into desktop application development, let's build a very simple GUI app using **Swing**.

Project Hello GUI

This project will show a small window with a button. When the button is clicked, a message appears.

```java
import javax.swing.*;

public class Main {
    public static void main(String[] args) {
        // Schedule a job for the event-dispatching
thread
        SwingUtilities.invokeLater(() ->
createAndShowGUI());
    }

    private static void createAndShowGUI() {
        // Create the frame (window)
        JFrame frame = new JFrame("Hello GUI!");

frame.setDefaultCloseOperation(JFrame.EXIT_ON_CLOSE);
        frame.setSize(300, 200);

        // Create a button
        JButton button = new JButton("Click Me!");

        // Add action to the button
        button.addActionListener(e ->
JOptionPane.showMessageDialog(frame, "Hello, Java GUI
World!"));

        // Add the button to the frame
        frame.getContentPane().add(button);

        // Display the frame
        frame.setVisible(true);
    }
}
```

Code Breakdown

Let's walk through what's happening

Code Segment	Explanation
`JFrame frame = new JFrame("Hello GUI!")`	This creates a window with the title "Hello GUI!".
`frame.setDefaultCloseOperation(...)`	Ensures the app closes properly when the window is closed.
`JButton button = new JButton("Click Me!")`	Creates a clickable button.
`button.addActionListener(...)`	Attaches an event so that when the button is clicked, a message pops up.
`frame.getContentPane().add(button)`	Adds the button to the frame's content area.

Code Segment	Explanation
`frame.setVisible(true)`	Makes the window visible on the screen.

Here's a simple **diagram** of the component hierarchy

```
[ JFrame ]
  └── [ JButton  "Click Me!" ]
```

Try It Yourself

Modify the program to do the following

- Change the button text to "Surprise Me!"
- Make the window larger
- Display your name instead of "Hello, Java GUI World!"

These small experiments are the seeds of mastery. As you tweak parameters and modify elements, you'll gain fluency in how Java GUIs work.

1.5 What's Next?

In the next chapter, we'll expand our understanding of layout managers and event handling. You'll build your own **calculator app** using Swing, exploring how multiple components can be arranged and how input can be processed in real time.

This chapter was a simple taste, but what you've just built is a working desktop application. You've installed your toolchain, written Java code, and interacted with GUI components—solid foundations for everything that follows.

And remember The best way to learn code is to **write** it. Don't just copy-paste—experiment, break things, and fix them. Build your own versions. Rename buttons. Resize windows. Make it yours.

Let the journey begin.

Chapter 2

Java Fundamentals Refresher

2.1 Why a Strong Foundation Matters

Before diving deep into graphical user interfaces, event-driven programming, and file-handling with Swing or JavaFX, it's critical to solidify your understanding of Java's core concepts. Think of these fundamentals as the internal wiring of a building—unseen by users but essential for everything to function correctly.

In this chapter, we'll take a focused yet expansive look at key elements of Java data types, conditionals, loops, arrays, functions (methods), object-oriented programming (OOP), exception handling, and packages. But this won't be a mere review—we'll apply what we learn in the form of two hands-on micro-projects a **Basic Calculator App** and a **Simple Contact Data Model**, each building your skills toward full-feature desktop applications.

2.2 Data Types and Variables

In Java, every piece of data has a **type**, and every type has specific **memory size**, **operations**, and **use cases**. Java is a **strongly typed language**, which means that you must declare the type of every variable before using it.

Here's a table summarizing Java's most commonly used primitive data types

Data Type	Size	Description	Example
int	4 bytes	Integer numbers	int age = 30;
double	8 bytes	Floating-point numbers	double pi = 3.1415;
char	2 bytes	A single character	char grade = 'A';
boolean	1 bit	True or false	boolean isOn = true;
String	varies	Text (not primitive, but used often)	String name = "Java";

When creating GUI-based applications, most data the user interacts with—text, numbers, selections—will need to be stored in variables. Imagine you're writing a calculator every number a user enters gets stored in a variable. So understanding how and when to use the right data type is key.

2.3 Conditional Statements

Conditions allow programs to make **decisions**. In GUI programs, conditions are everywhere "If the button is clicked, do this..." or "If the input is valid, then proceed."

```
int age = 20;

if (age >= 18) {
    System.out.println("You are eligible to vote.");
} else {
    System.out.println("You are not eligible.");
}
```

You can also use `switch-case` for handling multiple conditions

```
int option = 2;

switch(option) {
    case 1
        System.out.println("Option 1 selected.");
        break;
    case 2
        System.out.println("Option 2 selected.");
        break;
    default
        System.out.println("Unknown option.");
}
```

In GUI applications, switch-case is especially handy for menu selections or tab navigation.

2.4 Loops – The Engine of Repetition

Loops let you repeat actions without rewriting code. You'll use loops when displaying lists of data, updating interfaces, or validating inputs.

```
// For loop
for (int i = 0; i < 5; i++) {
    System.out.println("Iteration  " + i);
}
// While loop
int counter = 0;
while (counter < 3) {
    System.out.println("Counter is  " + counter);
    counter++;
}
```

Imagine looping through a list of contacts and displaying them in a table—this is where loops come in.

2.5 Arrays and Collections

Arrays store **multiple values of the same type**. This is perfect for apps that need to manage lists—like a contact manager or to-do list.

```
String[] names = {"Alice", "Bob", "Charlie"};
for (String name   names) {
    System.out.println("Name  " + name);
```

```
}
```

Here's a basic diagram to visualize an array

Index	0	1	2
Names	Alice	Bob	Charlie

Later, we'll transition to more dynamic data structures like `ArrayList`, which allows adding/removing items more flexibly.

2.6 Methods Reusable Code Blocks

Methods (or functions) let you organize your code into reusable chunks. In GUI apps, methods are used for handling events, updating UI, and separating logic from interface design.

```
public static int add(int a, int b) {
    return a + b;
}
```

Using the method

```
int result = add(10, 20);
System.out.println("Sum  " + result);
```

This becomes useful when designing buttons each button click can trigger a method with specific logic.

2.7 Object-Oriented Programming (OOP)

Java is inherently object-oriented. That means everything is modeled as **objects** that contain both **data** and **behavior**.

Key Concepts of OOP

Concept	Description
Class	A blueprint for creating objects
Object	An instance of a class
Encapsulation	Wrapping data and methods inside a class
Inheritance	Creating new classes based on existing ones
Polymorphism	One interface, many implementations

Here's a simple class for a contact

```java
public class Contact {
    String name;
    String phone;

    public Contact(String name, String phone) {
        this.name = name;
        this.phone = phone;
    }

    public void printContact() {
        System.out.println(name + "   " + phone);
    }
}
```

Creating and using objects

```java
Contact c1 = new Contact("Alice", "1234567890");
c1.printContact();
```

This will later serve as the foundation for our contact manager GUI application.

2.8 Exception Handling

When your program crashes because of invalid user input or a missing file, you need to **gracefully handle** those errors.

```java
try {
    int a = 10 / 0;
} catch (ArithmeticException e) {
    System.out.println("You can't divide by zero!");
}
```

You'll be using exception handling frequently when working with file I/O, database access, or GUI events.

2.9 Packages Organizing Code

Packages help you organize related classes into logical groups. Think of them as folders in your project.

To define a package

```
package myapp.models;

public class Contact { ... }
```

And to use it

```
import myapp.models.Contact;
```

This becomes especially useful in large desktop applications with many components (like models, services, UI, etc.).

2.10 Basic Calculator (Console-Based)

Let's tie the above concepts together by creating a **console-based calculator**. This isn't GUI yet—but it lays the logical groundwork.

```
import java.util.Scanner;

public class Calculator {
    public static void main(String[] args) {
```

```java
        Scanner input = new Scanner(System.in);

        System.out.print("Enter first number  ");
        double num1 = input.nextDouble();

        System.out.print("Enter operation (+, -, *,
/)  ");
        char op = input.next().charAt(0);

        System.out.print("Enter second number  ");
        double num2 = input.nextDouble();

        double result = 0;
        boolean valid = true;

        switch(op) {
            case '+'  result = num1 + num2; break;
            case '-'  result = num1 - num2; break;
            case '*'  result = num1 * num2; break;
            case '/'
                if (num2 != 0) result = num1 / num2;
                else {
                    System.out.println("Error  Divide
by zero");
                    valid = false;
                }
                break;
            default
                System.out.println("Invalid
operation");
                valid = false;
        }

        if (valid) System.out.println("Result  " +
result);
    }
}
```

Key Skills Reinforced

- Data types (double, char)
- Input handling
- Conditionals (switch)
- Exception prevention (if num2 != 0)
- Method structure and modular design (you can refactor the calculator operations into separate methods later)

2.11 Contact Data Model (OOP Practice)

Now let's build a **simple contact model** to practice object-oriented concepts. This will later connect directly to a GUI-based contact manager.

```java
public class Contact {
    private String name;
    private String phone;

    public Contact(String name, String phone) {
        this.name = name;
        this.phone = phone;
    }

    public String getName() {
        return name;
    }

    public String getPhone() {
        return phone;
    }

    public void printContact() {
        System.out.println("Name   " + name + ", Phone
" + phone);
    }
}
```

And here's how you might use this in a test class

```
public class ContactManager {
    public static void main(String[] args) {
        Contact c1 = new Contact("Alice",
"1234567890");
        Contact c2 = new Contact("Bob",
"9876543210");

        c1.printContact();
        c2.printContact();
    }
}
```

This model is intentionally kept minimal, but we'll add validation, file-saving, GUI interaction, and search functionality in future chapters.

2.12 Wrapping Up

You've just completed a robust refresher on Java's most essential building blocks. Each of these concepts—variables, loops, conditionals, functions, and OOP—is like a gear in the engine of your future applications. Without mastering these, the car won't run. But with them? You'll be speeding through app development with control and confidence.

The two hands-on projects have given you practical muscle memory. Don't skip writing these by hand. Type them, run them, tweak them, and break them. That's how mastery happens.

In the next chapter, we'll bring the **contact data model** to life in a **Swing-based contact manager GUI**, applying object-oriented concepts and interactive design to build something both functional and fun.

Let's keep building.

Chapter 3

Building Your First GUI App – Notepad Clone

3.1 The Power of a Practical Project

Welcome to your first real graphical user interface project in Java a full-fledged Notepad clone. By the end of this chapter, you'll not only know how to write code that looks and feels like an application but you'll also learn the critical thinking that goes into constructing software people can use.

A Notepad may seem simple on the surface, but its development requires a solid understanding of Java Swing, event-driven programming, file input/output operations, layout managers, and text component behaviors. You'll be learning concepts that are transferrable to larger-scale projects such as code editors, writing tools, or report managers. And most importantly, you'll get your hands dirty writing actual code that works.

Let's begin by setting the groundwork.

3.2 Introduction to Java Swing

Java Swing is a part of the Java Foundation Classes (JFC) that provides a rich set of GUI components. Swing is lightweight, platform-independent, and built entirely in Java. Unlike older AWT (Abstract Window Toolkit) components, Swing components are written purely in Java and offer a pluggable look and feel.

The core class for building any GUI in Swing is `JFrame`, which acts as the main window of your application. Everything visible—buttons, menus, text areas—gets added to this frame.

Below is a diagram to illustrate the basic component hierarchy of a Swing-based GUI

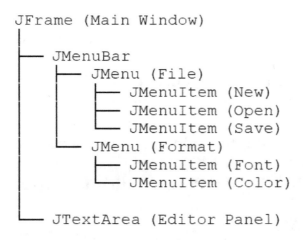

```
JFrame (Main Window)
|
├── JMenuBar
|    ├── JMenu (File)
|    |    ├── JMenuItem (New)
|    |    ├── JMenuItem (Open)
|    |    └── JMenuItem (Save)
|    └── JMenu (Format)
|         ├── JMenuItem (Font)
|         └── JMenuItem (Color)
|
└── JTextArea (Editor Panel)
```

Now, let's translate this structure into a functioning Java program.

3.3 Step-by-Step Implementation of Notepad Clone

Let us now build the full app step by step. Please follow along with the code and explanations. Don't copy-paste—type and tweak it for deeper learning.

Step 1 Creating the Main Window

```java
import javax.swing.*;

public class NotepadApp {
    public static void main(String[] args) {
        SwingUtilities.invokeLater(() -> {
            new NotepadFrame();
        });
    }
}
```

The invokeLater() method ensures the UI updates are handled safely on the Event Dispatch Thread (EDT), the main thread responsible for all GUI rendering in Swing.

Now, we create the main NotepadFrame class.

Step 2 Building the JFrame with a TextArea

```java
import javax.swing.*;
import java.awt.*;

public class NotepadFrame extends JFrame {

    JTextArea textArea;

    public NotepadFrame() {
        setTitle("Java Notepad");
        setSize(800, 600);
        setDefaultCloseOperation(EXIT_ON_CLOSE);

        textArea = new JTextArea();
        textArea.setFont(new Font("Arial",
Font.PLAIN, 16));
```

```
        JScrollPane scrollPane = new
JScrollPane(textArea);
        add(scrollPane);

        createMenuBar();

        setVisible(true);
    }
}
```

We initialize the `JTextArea` as the core component for editing text. A `JScrollPane` is wrapped around the `textArea` to support scrolling when content exceeds the screen.

3.4 Adding Menus and Menu Items

Menus are implemented using `JMenuBar`, `JMenu`, and `JMenuItem`.

```
private void createMenuBar() {
    JMenuBar menuBar = new JMenuBar();

    JMenu fileMenu = new JMenu("File");
    JMenuItem newItem = new JMenuItem("New");
    JMenuItem openItem = new JMenuItem("Open");
    JMenuItem saveItem = new JMenuItem("Save");

    fileMenu.add(newItem);
    fileMenu.add(openItem);
    fileMenu.add(saveItem);

    JMenu formatMenu = new JMenu("Format");
    JMenuItem fontItem = new JMenuItem("Font");
    JMenuItem colorItem = new JMenuItem("Color");
```

```
formatMenu.add(fontItem);
formatMenu.add(colorItem);

menuBar.add(fileMenu);
menuBar.add(formatMenu);

setJMenuBar(menuBar);

// Add event listeners later
}
```

Diagram Menu Structure

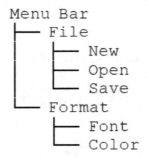

```
Menu Bar
├── File
│     ├── New
│     ├── Open
│     └── Save
└── Format
      ├── Font
      └── Color
```

3.5 File I/O with JFileChooser

Let's handle New, Open, and Save using file input/output
and JFileChooser.

Implementing "New"

```
newItem.addActionListener(e -> textArea.setText(""));
```

34

Implementing "Open"

```
openItem.addActionListener(e -> {
    JFileChooser fileChooser = new JFileChooser();
    int option = fileChooser.showOpenDialog(this);
    if (option == JFileChooser.APPROVE_OPTION) {
        try {
            File file =
fileChooser.getSelectedFile();
            Scanner scanner = new Scanner(file);
            StringBuilder content = new
StringBuilder();
            while (scanner.hasNextLine()) {

content.append(scanner.nextLine()).append("\n");
            }
            textArea.setText(content.toString());
            scanner.close();
        } catch (Exception ex) {
            JOptionPane.showMessageDialog(this,
"Error opening file  " + ex.getMessage());
        }
    }
});
```

Implementing "Save"

```
saveItem.addActionListener(e -> {
    JFileChooser fileChooser = new JFileChooser();
    int option = fileChooser.showSaveDialog(this);
    if (option == JFileChooser.APPROVE_OPTION) {
        try {
            FileWriter writer = new
FileWriter(fileChooser.getSelectedFile());
            writer.write(textArea.getText());
            writer.close();
        } catch (Exception ex) {
            JOptionPane.showMessageDialog(this,
"Error saving file  " + ex.getMessage());
```

```
        }
    }
});
```

This segment introduces readers to **persistent data**, a key concept in desktop apps.

3.6 Font and Color Formatting

Let's add basic formatting. We'll use `JColorChooser` and `JFontChooser` (a simple custom dialog).

Text Color Using JColorChooser

```
colorItem.addActionListener(e -> {
    Color color = JColorChooser.showDialog(this,
"Choose Text Color", textArea.getForeground());
    if (color != null) {
        textArea.setForeground(color);
    }
});
```

Font Selector (Simple Custom Dialog)

Unfortunately, Swing doesn't have a built-in `JFontChooser`. So let's build a minimal version using a modal dialog

```
fontItem.addActionListener(e -> {
    String[] fonts =
GraphicsEnvironment.getLocalGraphicsEnvironment().get
AvailableFontFamilyNames();
    String selectedFont = (String)
JOptionPane.showInputDialog(this, "Choose Font",
```

```
        "Font Picker", JOptionPane.PLAIN_MESSAGE,
null, fonts, textArea.getFont().getFamily());
    if (selectedFont != null) {
        textArea.setFont(new Font(selectedFont,
Font.PLAIN, 16));
    }
});
```

3.7 Summary of Components Learned

Component	Role in Notepad Clone
JFrame	Main window
JTextArea	Editable text box
JMenuBar	Top-level container for menus
JMenu	Menu like File or Format
JMenuItem	Selectable menu options
JScrollPane	Makes text area scrollable
JFileChooser	File open/save dialogs

Component	Role in Notepad Clone
JColorChooser	Allows users to pick a color
JOptionPane	Pop-up input or error messages

3.8 Final Code Structure and Execution Flow

Here is the simplified class structure and flow

```
NotepadApp.java
  └── launches NotepadFrame ()

NotepadFrame.java
  ├── Initializes GUI
  ├── Loads MenuBar
  ├── Attaches Listeners for File and Format actions
  └── Manages TextArea and I/O
```

The program begins in `main()` and opens a window. From there, user interactions (like clicking "Open" or "Save") trigger various actions through **event listeners**, which are small pieces of code that "listen" for events and react accordingly.

3.9 Exercises for the Reader

Now that you've built a functioning GUI app, take on the following modifications to deepen your skills

1. Add a "Word Count" menu item that shows how many words and characters are in the document.
2. Add support for changing font size using a slider.
3. Implement a "Find and Replace" feature using `JDialog` and string operations.
4. Add a status bar showing file path and last saved time.

This chapter marked your first serious venture into real-world desktop applications using Java. You didn't just read about menus, text editors, and file operations—you built them. From understanding the layout of a Swing window to handling file input and customizing fonts and colors, you've now crossed the bridge from abstract coding to concrete software creation. Most importantly, you now see that even complex-looking apps are built from small, understandable pieces. This project-based learning method not only strengthens your technical muscle but also teaches you how to **think like a software engineer**—by breaking big problems into solvable parts. In the next chapter, we'll scale this further by incorporating **data persistence using files and search functionality**, and eventually transition to building **multi-window applications**. But for now, take a breath, admire your work, and maybe type a few words into your new notepad. You've earned it.

Chapter 4

Build a Task Manager App with Save & Load

4.1 Learning by Building Why a Task Manager?

Few applications are as universally useful—and deceptively complex—as a personal task manager. At first glance, it seems simple write down tasks, mark them done, and maybe group them into categories. But from a software development perspective, this app introduces you to a wealth of fundamental and advanced concepts. These include custom data modeling, user interface (UI) design, event-driven interaction, file persistence, layout management, and the use of serialization or JSON for saving data.

In this chapter, we are going to architect, build, and refine a fully functioning **To-Do List Application** using **Java Swing**. You'll learn not just how to code it, but how to **think** about building such applications in a modular, extensible way. This is hands-on, practical learning—the kind that embeds skills deep into your developer muscle memory.

4.2 Functional Goals and Feature Set

Before we dive into coding, it is essential to understand the functional blueprint of our Task Manager. The app will consist of the following key features

• A text input for entering tasks

- A drop-down (combo box) to choose task categories
- A checkbox to mark tasks as completed
- A table to display all tasks
- Buttons to add, delete, and save/load tasks
- File I/O to persist task data using **Java serialization** or **JSON format**

4.3 Modeling the Task Object

Let us begin with the building blocks—data. Each task should encapsulate a **description**, a **category**, and a **completed flag**. For this, we create a Java class named Task.

Code Task.java

```
import java.io.Serializable;

public class Task implements Serializable {
    private String description;
    private String category;
    private boolean completed;

    public Task(String description, String category,
boolean completed) {
        this.description = description;
        this.category = category;
        this.completed = completed;
    }

    public String getDescription() {
        return description;
    }

    public String getCategory() {
        return category;
```

```
    }

    public boolean isCompleted() {
        return completed;
    }

    public void setCompleted(boolean completed) {
        this.completed = completed;
    }

    @Override
    public String toString() {
        return description + " [" + category + "]";
    }
}
```

Here, Serializable allows us to save and load tasks via binary files. Later, we'll also explore JSON as a more human-readable format.

4.4 Designing the GUI with Swing Components

Now let's build the application's user interface using advanced Swing components such as JComboBox, JTable, JCheckBox, and layout managers.

Main Frame Structure TaskManagerApp.java

```
import javax.swing.*;
import java.awt.*;
import java.util.ArrayList;

public class TaskManagerApp extends JFrame {
    private ArrayList<Task> tasks = new
ArrayList<>();
    private JTable taskTable;
```

```java
    private TaskTableModel tableModel;

    public TaskManagerApp() {
        setTitle("Task Manager");
        setSize(700, 400);
        setDefaultCloseOperation(EXIT_ON_CLOSE);
        setLayout(new BorderLayout());

        add(createInputPanel(), BorderLayout.NORTH);
        add(createTablePanel(), BorderLayout.CENTER);
        add(createButtonPanel(), BorderLayout.SOUTH);

        setVisible(true);
    }

    // Will define createInputPanel(),
createTablePanel(), and createButtonPanel() below
}
```

This uses `BorderLayout` to split the window into logical regions.

4.5 Input Panel – Task Entry

```java
private JTextField taskField;
private JComboBox<String> categoryCombo;

private JPanel createInputPanel() {
    JPanel panel = new JPanel();
    panel.setLayout(new FlowLayout());

    taskField = new JTextField(20);
    categoryCombo = new JComboBox<>(new
String[]{"Personal", "Work", "School", "Other"});

    JButton addButton = new JButton("Add Task");
    addButton.addActionListener(e -> addTask());

    panel.add(new JLabel("Task "));
    panel.add(taskField);
```

```
panel.add(categoryCombo);
panel.add(addButton);

return panel;
}
```

The JComboBox allows users to choose a category. When the button is clicked, it triggers addTask() to insert a new task into the list.

4.6 Table Panel – Display Tasks

We'll create a custom table model using AbstractTableModel to hold our tasks in a table with checkboxes for completion.

Code TaskTableModel.java

```java
import javax.swing.table.AbstractTableModel;
import java.util.List;

public class TaskTableModel extends
AbstractTableModel {
    private final String[] columns = {"Done",
"Description", "Category"};
    private final List<Task> taskList;

    public TaskTableModel(List<Task> tasks) {
        this.taskList = tasks;
    }

    @Override
    public int getRowCount() {
        return taskList.size();
    }
```

```java
    @Override
    public int getColumnCount() {
        return columns.length;
    }

    @Override
    public Object getValueAt(int row, int col) {
        Task task = taskList.get(row);
        switch (col) {
            case 0   return task.isCompleted();
            case 1   return task.getDescription();
            case 2   return task.getCategory();
            default   return null;
        }
    }

    @Override
    public boolean isCellEditable(int row, int col) {
        return col == 0;
    }

    @Override
    public void setValueAt(Object value, int row, int
col) {
        if (col == 0) {
            taskList.get(row).setCompleted((Boolean)
value);
            fireTableCellUpdated(row, col);
        }
    }

    @Override
    public String getColumnName(int col) {
        return columns[col];
    }

    @Override
    public Class<?> getColumnClass(int col) {
        return (col == 0) ? Boolean.class
String.class;
```

```
    }
}
```

In `TaskManagerApp`, link this table model

```
private JPanel createTablePanel() {
    tableModel = new TaskTableModel(tasks);
    taskTable = new JTable(tableModel);
    return new JScrollPane(taskTable);
}
```

4.7 Bottom Panel – Save and Load Buttons

```
private JPanel createButtonPanel() {
    JPanel panel = new JPanel();
    panel.setLayout(new FlowLayout());

    JButton saveButton = new JButton("Save Tasks");
    JButton loadButton = new JButton("Load Tasks");

    saveButton.addActionListener(e -> saveTasks());
    loadButton.addActionListener(e -> loadTasks());

    panel.add(saveButton);
    panel.add(loadButton);
    return panel;
}
```

4.8 Save and Load Logic with Serialization

Here's how to save and load using Java's built-in `ObjectOutputStream`.

```
private void saveTasks() {
    try (ObjectOutputStream out = new
ObjectOutputStream(new
FileOutputStream("tasks.ser"))) {
        out.writeObject(tasks);
```

```
        JOptionPane.showMessageDialog(this, "Tasks
saved!");
    } catch (Exception e) {
        JOptionPane.showMessageDialog(this, "Error
saving tasks  " + e.getMessage());
    }
}

private void loadTasks() {
    try (ObjectInputStream in = new
ObjectInputStream(new FileInputStream("tasks.ser")))
{
        tasks.clear();
        tasks.addAll((ArrayList<Task>)
in.readObject());
        tableModel.fireTableDataChanged();
        JOptionPane.showMessageDialog(this, "Tasks
loaded!");
    } catch (Exception e) {
        JOptionPane.showMessageDialog(this, "Error
loading tasks  " + e.getMessage());
    }
}
```

Now your users' data persists across sessions—your Task Manager remembers!

4.9 Optional JSON Save and Load with GSON

To offer a more human-readable format, use the Google GSON library.

```
Gson gson = new Gson();
String json = gson.toJson(tasks);
FileWriter writer = new FileWriter("tasks.json");
writer.write(json);
writer.close();
```

And for loading

```
Reader reader = new FileReader("tasks.json");
Type taskListType = new
TypeToken<ArrayList<Task>>(){}.getType();
tasks = gson.fromJson(reader, taskListType);
```

This opens up future interoperability with web or mobile apps.

4.10 Final Application Structure

```
/TaskManagerApp.java      // Main application GUI
/Task.java                // Serializable Task
model
/TaskTableModel.java      // Custom table logic
/tasks.ser                // Serialized binary file
/tasks.json               // Optional JSON backup
```

4.11 Project Expansion Challenges

Now that you've completed the core app, consider adding

- Due dates using JDatePicker
- Filter by category using JComboBox at the bottom
- Data export to Excel using Apache POI
- Cloud sync with REST API

In this chapter, you built a real desktop productivity tool that can organize your daily work—and in doing so, you gained mastery over several critical desktop development skills in Java. You modeled objects, handled file persistence, learned about JTable, used

49

advanced Swing components, and even introduced user customization. You didn't just code—you engineered a product.

Now you're ready to build more ambitious tools. The next chapter will guide you through building a **Multi-Window Address Book Application**, where we'll go deeper into event communication between windows, and explore custom dialogs and component reusability. Your desktop development journey has just begun. Get some coffee. You deserve it.

Chapter 5

Personal Finance Tracker – Learn File I/O and Data Models

5.1 Why Build a Finance Tracker?

Money matters. Whether you're a student managing lunch expenses or a professional monitoring multiple accounts, having a personal finance tracker helps bring clarity and control. From a software development standpoint, building such an application is the perfect way to introduce core concepts such as **custom class design**, **data modeling**, **file I/O using CSV**, and **data visualization with charts**.

In this chapter, you will build a **Personal Finance Tracker** desktop application in Java using Swing. This project integrates several intermediate and advanced features of desktop application development, including modular class architecture, file import/export mechanisms using CSV format, and dynamic chart generation using **JFreeChart**.

5.2 Application Overview

The Finance Tracker application we will build enables users to do the following

- Add, edit, and delete income and expense transactions
- Categorize each transaction (e.g., Food, Rent, Salary, Entertainment)
- Store transactions in memory and save them as CSV files

- Load transactions from existing CSV files
- View financial summaries with pie chart visualizations

The application's UI is structured into three major panels a **Transaction Entry Panel**, a **Transaction Table**, and a **Summary & Chart Panel**.

5.3 Designing the Data Model Accounts

Let's begin by defining the data structures that will power our application. Unlike toy examples, this project teaches you how to plan and abstract real-world objects into reusable classes.

We'll create the following core classes

- `Transaction` Represents a financial transaction.
- `TransactionType` An enum to differentiate between income and expense.
- `Category` A string field to categorize each transaction.
- `TransactionManager` Manages the collection of all transactions, calculates summaries, and handles CSV file operations.

Code TransactionType.java

```java
public enum TransactionType {
    INCOME,
    EXPENSE
}
```

Code Transaction.java

```java
import java.io.Serializable;
import java.time.LocalDate;

public class Transaction implements Serializable {
    private String description;
    private double amount;
    private String category;
    private TransactionType type;
    private LocalDate date;

    public Transaction(String description, double
amount, String category, TransactionType type,
LocalDate date) {
        this.description = description;
        this.amount = amount;
        this.category = category;
        this.type = type;
        this.date = date;
    }

    public double getSignedAmount() {
        return type == TransactionType.EXPENSE ? -
amount    amount;
    }

    // Getters and setters omitted for brevity
}
```

Code TransactionManager.java

```java
import java.util.ArrayList;
import java.util.List;
import java.util.Map;
import java.util.HashMap;

public class TransactionManager {
```

```java
    private final List<Transaction> transactions =
new ArrayList<>();

    public void addTransaction(Transaction t) {
        transactions.add(t);
    }

    public List<Transaction> getAllTransactions() {
        return transactions;
    }

    public Map<String, Double> getCategorySummary() {
        Map<String, Double> summary = new
HashMap<>();
        for (Transaction t   transactions) {
            String cat = t.getCategory();
            double amt = t.getSignedAmount();
            summary.put(cat,
summary.getOrDefault(cat, 0.0) + amt);
        }
        return summary;
    }
}
```

5.4 Building the GUI Java Swing in Action

The GUI is designed with JTextField for descriptions and amounts, JComboBox for category selection, JRadioButton for type selection (income or expense), a JTable for displaying transactions, and a custom panel for pie charts.

Let's begin with the input form.

Code Snippet Entry Panel UI

```java
private JPanel createEntryPanel() {
    JPanel panel = new JPanel(new FlowLayout());

    descriptionField = new JTextField(15);
    amountField = new JTextField(10);
    categoryCombo = new JComboBox<>(new
String[]{"Food", "Rent", "Salary", "Entertainment",
"Other"});

    incomeRadio = new JRadioButton("Income", true);
    expenseRadio = new JRadioButton("Expense");
    ButtonGroup typeGroup = new ButtonGroup();
    typeGroup.add(incomeRadio);
    typeGroup.add(expenseRadio);

    JButton addButton = new JButton("Add
Transaction");
    addButton.addActionListener(e ->
addTransaction());

    panel.add(new JLabel("Description "));
    panel.add(descriptionField);
    panel.add(new JLabel("Amount "));
    panel.add(amountField);
    panel.add(categoryCombo);
    panel.add(incomeRadio);
    panel.add(expenseRadio);
    panel.add(addButton);

    return panel;
}
```

The `addTransaction()` method reads input, constructs a new `Transaction`, and updates the table model accordingly.

5.5 Transaction Table and Model

Just like in the task manager app, we use a custom table model

```
public class FinanceTableModel extends
AbstractTableModel {
    private final String[] columns = {"Date",
"Description", "Category", "Type", "Amount"};
    private final List<Transaction> transactions;

    public FinanceTableModel(List<Transaction>
transactions) {
        this.transactions = transactions;
    }

    @Override
    public int getRowCount() {
        return transactions.size();
    }

    @Override
    public int getColumnCount() {
        return columns.length;
    }

    @Override
    public Object getValueAt(int row, int col) {
        Transaction t = transactions.get(row);
        return switch (col) {
            case 0 -> t.getDate();
            case 1 -> t.getDescription();
            case 2 -> t.getCategory();
            case 3 -> t.getType();
            case 4 -> t.getSignedAmount();
            default -> null;
        };
    }
```

```
    @Override
    public String getColumnName(int col) {
        return columns[col];
    }
}
```

5.6 CSV Export/Import Functions

Save Transactions to CSV

```
public void saveToCSV(String filename) throws
IOException {
    FileWriter writer = new FileWriter(filename);
    for (Transaction t    transactions) {

writer.write(String.format("%s,%s,%s,%s,%.2f%n",
                t.getDate(), t.getDescription(),
t.getCategory(),
                t.getType(), t.getSignedAmount()));
    }
    writer.close();
}
```

Load Transactions from CSV

```
public void loadFromCSV(String filename) throws
IOException {
    BufferedReader reader = new BufferedReader(new
FileReader(filename));
    String line;
    while ((line = reader.readLine()) != null) {
        String[] parts = line.split(",");
        LocalDate date = LocalDate.parse(parts[0]);
        String desc = parts[1];
        String cat = parts[2];
        TransactionType type =
TransactionType.valueOf(parts[3]);
        double amount = Double.parseDouble(parts[4]);
```

```
        transactions.add(new Transaction(desc,
Math.abs(amount), cat, type, date));
    }
    reader.close();
}
```

5.7 Pie Chart Visualization with JFreeChart

To create a dynamic pie chart showing spending by category, use JFreeChart. First, add the JFreeChart library to your project (via Maven or manually).

Code to Generate Pie Chart

```
public void showPieChart() {
    DefaultPieDataset dataset = new
DefaultPieDataset();
    Map<String, Double> summary =
transactionManager.getCategorySummary();

    for (Map.Entry<String, Double> entry
summary.entrySet()) {
        if (entry.getValue() < 0) // Only expenses
            dataset.setValue(entry.getKey(),
Math.abs(entry.getValue()));
    }

    JFreeChart chart = ChartFactory.createPieChart(
        "Spending by Category",
        dataset,
        true, true, false
    );

    ChartPanel chartPanel = new ChartPanel(chart);
    JFrame chartFrame = new JFrame("Expense
Summary");
    chartFrame.setContentPane(chartPanel);
    chartFrame.pack();
```

```
    chartFrame.setVisible(true);
}
```

5.8 Suggested Enhancements

Once you finish this project, you can expand your app in multiple directions

- Support multiple users or account types
- Add recurring transactions
- Use an embedded database like SQLite
- Build a reporting module with bar graphs for monthly trends

You've just completed a fully functional **Personal Finance Tracker**, one that demonstrates your grasp of Java file I/O, class modeling, data handling, and visual representation. You've learned how to handle external file formats, how to build structured data models that reflect real-world entities, and how to visualize user data in compelling ways.

This is not just a program—it's a professional-grade tool. And you built it.

In the next chapter, we will further elevate your skills by constructing a **multi-tabbed media library** where you'll manage and preview songs and video metadata. We'll introduce Java multimedia integration, file selection dialogs, and threading. Keep going—you're gaining serious developer firepower.

Chapter 6

Password Vault App with Encryption

6.1 Why Build a Password Vault?

In an age where data breaches have become alarmingly common, one of the most crucial skills any developer can acquire is understanding **secure software design**. Users need safe places to store passwords, and developers must be able to provide that without compromising usability or functionality.

This chapter challenges you to design and build a **Password Vault Application**—a secure desktop app where users can store credentials such as usernames and passwords for various services like email, bank accounts, or social media. What makes this project powerful is that it teaches you to handle **sensitive data responsibly**, using real-world **encryption**, **hashing**, and **file security** strategies.

The core technology used for encryption in this chapter will be Java's `javax.crypto` package. We'll explore the **AES (Advanced Encryption Standard)** symmetric encryption method and **SHA-256 hashing** to safeguard master passwords. You will not only build a working application but will also develop the awareness to evaluate security trade-offs in future software you build.

6.2 Application Blueprint and Workflow

Before we start coding, it's essential to understand the big picture of how the application works. Here's a high-level breakdown

6.3 Concepts of Security Hashing Explained

What is Hashing?

Hashing is a one-way cryptographic function used to validate information. In our app, we'll hash the **master password** using **SHA-256**, which means even if someone gains access to the hashed value, they can't reverse-engineer the actual password. When the user enters a password later, we hash the input again and compare it with the stored hash.

What is Encryption?

Unlike hashing, encryption is reversible. We'll use **AES symmetric encryption**, which means the same password (key) is used to both encrypt and decrypt data. This will be used to securely store and retrieve user credentials from the vault.

Here's a basic comparison

Function	Hashing	Encryption
Direction	One-way	Two-way (encrypt/decrypt)
Reversible?	No	Yes
Use Case	Password storage	Data protection (credentials)
Java Class	MessageDigest	Cipher

6.4 Project Setup and Tools

You will need

- Java Development Kit (JDK) 11 or higher

- IntelliJ IDEA or Eclipse IDE
- JCE (Java Cryptography Extension) – included in modern JDKs

The UI will be constructed with Java Swing. We'll need a few files for storing data

- `vault.dat` Encrypted credential storage
- `master.hash` Stores the SHA-256 hashed master password

6.5 Step-by-Step Code Walkthrough

Step 1 Creating the Master Password Setup

The very first time the application is run, it should ask the user to create a master password. This password is hashed using SHA-256 and stored in a file called `master.hash`.

```
import java.security.MessageDigest;
import java.nio.file.*;
import java.util.Base64;

public class MasterPasswordManager {
    private static final String HASH_FILE =
"master.hash";

    public static void saveMasterPassword(String
password) throws Exception {
        MessageDigest digest =
MessageDigest.getInstance("SHA-256");
        byte[] hashed =
digest.digest(password.getBytes("UTF-8"));
```

```
        String base64Hash =
Base64.getEncoder().encodeToString(hashed);
        Files.write(Paths.get(HASH_FILE),
base64Hash.getBytes());
    }

    public static boolean validatePassword(String
input) throws Exception {
        byte[] storedHash =
Files.readAllBytes(Paths.get(HASH_FILE));
        MessageDigest digest =
MessageDigest.getInstance("SHA-256");
        byte[] inputHash =
digest.digest(input.getBytes("UTF-8"));
        String inputBase64 =
Base64.getEncoder().encodeToString(inputHash);
        return inputBase64.equals(new
String(storedHash));
    }

    public static boolean isFirstRun() {
        return !Files.exists(Paths.get(HASH_FILE));
    }
}
```

Step 2 Vault Entry Data Model

We now define our core model the credential entry.

```
public class VaultEntry implements Serializable {
    private String service;
    private String username;
    private String password;  // This will be
encrypted before storage

    public VaultEntry(String service, String
username, String password) {
        this.service = service;
        this.username = username;
```

```java
        this.password = password;
    }

    // Getters and setters omitted for brevity
}
```

Step 3 AES Encryption Utilities

```java
import javax.crypto.*;
import javax.crypto.spec.SecretKeySpec;
import java.security.MessageDigest;
import java.util.Base64;

public class EncryptionUtil {
    private static SecretKeySpec getKey(String
password) throws Exception {
        byte[] key = password.getBytes("UTF-8");
        MessageDigest sha =
MessageDigest.getInstance("SHA-256");
        key = sha.digest(key);
        return new SecretKeySpec(key, "AES");
    }

    public static String encrypt(String strToEncrypt,
String secret) throws Exception {
        SecretKeySpec secretKey = getKey(secret);
        Cipher cipher = Cipher.getInstance("AES");
        cipher.init(Cipher.ENCRYPT_MODE, secretKey);
        return
Base64.getEncoder().encodeToString(cipher.doFinal(str
ToEncrypt.getBytes("UTF-8")));
    }

    public static String decrypt(String strToDecrypt,
String secret) throws Exception {
        SecretKeySpec secretKey = getKey(secret);
        Cipher cipher = Cipher.getInstance("AES");
        cipher.init(Cipher.DECRYPT_MODE, secretKey);
```

```
        return new
String(cipher.doFinal(Base64.getDecoder().decode(strT
oDecrypt)));
    }
}
```

6.6 Saving and Loading Vault Data Securely

Instead of storing plain `VaultEntry` objects, we serialize and encrypt them.

```
public class VaultFileManager {
    private static final String VAULT_FILE =
"vault.dat";

    public static void saveVault(List<VaultEntry>
entries, String masterPassword) throws Exception {
        ByteArrayOutputStream baos = new
ByteArrayOutputStream();
        ObjectOutputStream oos = new
ObjectOutputStream(baos);
        oos.writeObject(entries);
        oos.close();
        String encryptedData =
EncryptionUtil.encrypt(Base64.getEncoder().encodeToSt
ring(baos.toByteArray()), masterPassword);
        Files.write(Paths.get(VAULT_FILE),
encryptedData.getBytes());
    }

    public static List<VaultEntry> loadVault(String
masterPassword) throws Exception {
        byte[] encryptedBytes =
Files.readAllBytes(Paths.get(VAULT_FILE));
        String decryptedData =
EncryptionUtil.decrypt(new String(encryptedBytes),
masterPassword);
        byte[] objectData =
Base64.getDecoder().decode(decryptedData);
```

```
        ObjectInputStream ois = new
ObjectInputStream(new
ByteArrayInputStream(objectData));
        return (List<VaultEntry>) ois.readObject();
    }
}
```

6.7 Creating the User Interface

The interface has two primary states

1. **Login/Setup Window**
2. **Main Vault Panel** with a table of entries and an
   "Add Entry" dialog

Each entry consists of the **service name**, **username**,
and **password**, and can be viewed or hidden using a
"show/hide" toggle. You may use `JPasswordField`,
`JTextField`, `JTable`, and `JDialog` components to create
this interface.

6.8 Suggested Challenges for Readers

Once you've finished the core password vault
application, you can challenge yourself to implement
the following

- Add a password generator tool with complexity
  options (length, symbols, digits).
- Implement automatic logout after X minutes of
  inactivity.

- Add encrypted clipboard copy functionality with timeout.
- Store data in an embedded database (e.g., H2 or SQLite with encrypted tables).
- Sync vault data to a cloud service securely with OAuth.

In this chapter, you've built a fully encrypted Password Vault desktop app using Java Swing and Java Cryptography APIs. More importantly, you've crossed the line from "developer" to someone who thinks like a security engineer. You've learned the core principles of hashing, AES encryption, data serialization, and vault-style UI development. These skills are vital for any developer aiming to work with sensitive information or simply build reliable, safe tools for users.

In the next chapter, we'll explore **Media Library Management**—a project where you'll integrate media metadata scanning, file previews, tagging, and smart sorting systems. We'll use background threading and explore external libraries like Apache Tika for content parsing. Keep building. You're not just learning Java—you're building a developer mindset.

Chapter 7

Build a Desktop Alarm Clock & Timer

7.1 Introduction Why Build an Alarm Clock App?

At first glance, building a desktop alarm clock might seem like a simple project. But dig a little deeper and you'll discover it's a miniature ecosystem of real-world problems that mirror larger application development **time-based event handling, threading, user interaction, system integration, sound handling, and notifications**.

An alarm clock application is not just about setting alarms. It also includes managing **repeating tasks**, **triggering audio notifications**, **handling multithreaded behavior**, and **ensuring the GUI remains responsive** during background operations. Building this project will give you solid exposure to **timers**, **Java concurrency**, **event-driven programming**, and **real-time task execution**—all critical concepts for anyone aspiring to become a proficient software developer.

By the end of this chapter, you will have built a complete desktop-based Alarm Clock and Timer tool with the following features

- A simple, intuitive Swing GUI for setting alarms and countdown timers
- Notification popups and sound alerts when alarms go off

- The use of `javax.swing.Timer`, `java.util.Timer`, and background threads
- Scheduling reminders with custom messages
- Integration with the system tray to allow background operation

7.2 Functional Overview and Architecture

Let's begin with a functional breakdown of our application. The system will consist of three main modules that work in harmony

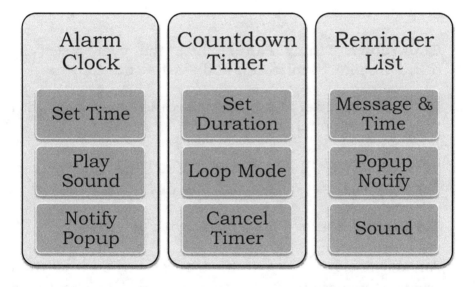

Each feature will be implemented with clean separation of logic, so you can extend, debug, or replace components easily.

We will use Swing for the UI, `Timer` classes for scheduling, `Thread` for long-running tasks, and `SystemTray` for background control.

7.3 Step 1 Designing the User Interface

A good user interface for an alarm clock must be simple, yet capable. The main application window should consist of three tabs or panels

Alarm Clock Panel Lets the user pick a time and activate/deactivate the alarm.

Countdown Timer Panel Lets the user specify a duration (like 10 minutes) and start a countdown.

Reminders Panel Displays scheduled messages with times and optional sound.

You can implement this layout using `JTabbedPane`, `JTextField`, `JSpinner`, `JButton`, and `JTable`.

7.4 Step 2 Alarm Clock Logic with Threads

An alarm clock waits until a specific time and then triggers an action. To do this, we need to check the current time against the set alarm time. A background thread ensures this doesn't freeze the UI.

```
public class AlarmTask implements Runnable {
    private LocalTime alarmTime;
```

```java
    private boolean running = true;
    private String message;

    public AlarmTask(LocalTime alarmTime, String
message) {
        this.alarmTime = alarmTime;
        this.message = message;
    }

    public void run() {
        while (running) {
            if
(LocalTime.now().withSecond(0).equals(alarmTime)) {
                showPopup(message);
                playSound();
                break;
            }
            try {
                Thread.sleep(1000); // check every
second
            } catch (InterruptedException e) {
                running = false;
            }
        }
    }

    public void cancel() {
        running = false;
    }

    private void showPopup(String msg) {
        JOptionPane.showMessageDialog(null, "ALARM   "
+ msg);
    }

    private void playSound() {
        try {
            File soundFile = new File("alarm.wav");
            AudioInputStream audio =
AudioSystem.getAudioInputStream(soundFile);
```

```
                Clip clip = AudioSystem.getClip();
                clip.open(audio);
                clip.start();
            } catch (Exception e) {
                e.printStackTrace();
            }
        }
    }
}
```

You can create and run this thread when the user clicks "Set Alarm." Make sure you store a reference so you can cancel it later.

7.5 Countdown Timer Using javax.swing.Timer

For countdown timers, a Swing Timer works well since it can run on the event dispatch thread and is easy to update UI components directly.

```
public class CountdownTimer {
    private Timer timer;
    private int secondsLeft;
    private JLabel display;

    public CountdownTimer(int seconds, JLabel
display) {
        this.secondsLeft = seconds;
        this.display = display;
        this.timer = new Timer(1000, e -> {
            secondsLeft--;
            updateDisplay();
            if (secondsLeft <= 0) {
                timer.stop();
                showPopup("Countdown Finished!");
                playSound();
            }
```

```
        });
    }

    public void start() {
        timer.start();
    }

    public void stop() {
        timer.stop();
    }

    private void updateDisplay() {
        int mins = secondsLeft / 60;
        int secs = secondsLeft % 60;
        display.setText(String.format("%02d %02d",
mins, secs));
    }

    private void showPopup(String msg) {
        JOptionPane.showMessageDialog(null, msg);
    }

    private void playSound() {
        // same sound logic as before
    }
}
```

This class is great for a visual timer that updates a label every second.

7.6 Step 4 Creating Reminder Scheduling

To implement scheduled reminders, we need a way to store a list of reminders and check if any of them should be fired. A `java.util.Timer` with a `TimerTask` works perfectly for this.

Create a class like

```java
public class Reminder {
    private String message;
    private LocalDateTime time;

    public Reminder(String message, LocalDateTime
time) {
        this.message = message;
        this.time = time;
    }

    public long delayUntilNow() {
        return Duration.between(LocalDateTime.now(),
time).toMillis();
    }
}
```

Then schedule them like this

```java
public class ReminderScheduler {
    private Timer timer = new Timer();

    public void schedule(Reminder reminder) {
        timer.schedule(new TimerTask() {
            public void run() {
                showPopup(reminder.getMessage());
                playSound();
            }
        }, reminder.delayUntilNow());
    }
}
```

7.7 System Tray Integration

You can keep your app running in the background by integrating it with the system tray. Java provides `java.awt.SystemTray` for this.

```
if (SystemTray.isSupported()) {
    SystemTray tray = SystemTray.getSystemTray();
    Image image =
Toolkit.getDefaultToolkit().getImage("clock.png");
    PopupMenu popup = new PopupMenu();
    MenuItem exitItem = new MenuItem("Exit");
    exitItem.addActionListener(e -> System.exit(0));
    popup.add(exitItem);
    TrayIcon trayIcon = new TrayIcon(image, "Alarm
Clock", popup);
    tray.add(trayIcon);
}
```

This allows the user to minimize the app and still get notifications and alarms without keeping the main window open.

7.8 Bringing It All Together

At this point, you will have a complete, functioning desktop utility that supports

- One-time and repeating alarms
- Countdown timers with UI updates
- Reminder scheduling
- System tray notifications
- Sound playback and popup alerts

- Threading and real-time updates

All of this is written using standard Java, without needing third-party frameworks.

7.9 Additional Features for Readers

To challenge your skills and expand the app, consider adding

- Saving and loading alarms and reminders from file (JSON or serialized objects)
- Support for recurring alarms (daily/weekly)
- Snooze functionality with rescheduling
- A dark mode UI theme
- Synchronization with Google Calendar using API

This chapter taught you far more than how to build a clock. You have learned to manage Java threads, utilize Swing timers for periodic tasks, manipulate the user interface responsively, and interact with OS-level features like sound playback and system trays. These skills are foundational for more advanced applications, whether it's a calendar tool, reminder app, or even parts of a productivity suite.

In the next chapter, we'll dive into media file management—tag parsing, directory scanning, previews, and more. Until then, keep your alarms set, your code running, and your mind curious.

Chapter 8

Turning Java into a Local Messenger

Welcome to Chapter 8, where we take Java beyond the boundaries of your own computer and allow it to speak—quite literally—over a local network. In this chapter, we'll build a chat-like desktop messaging app from scratch. The app will allow two or more users on the same network to communicate with each other, mimicking the functionality of early instant messengers. The skills you'll gain here are not just useful—they're foundational if you want to work with multiplayer games, IoT systems, peer-to-peer tools, or collaborative applications.

This project touches on critical computer science concepts client-server architecture, socket programming, threading, network streams, and concurrency. And just as importantly, you will build a complete desktop GUI using Java Swing that allows users to chat with ease. By the end of this chapter, your program will support multiple users connecting to a server, assigning nicknames, sending time-stamped messages, and saving chat history.

8.2 What Are Sockets and Why Should You Care?

In computing, a **socket** is like a telephone jack that allows software applications to send and receive data through a network. Java has a built-in `java.net` package which allows two machines (or processes) to communicate using `Socket` (client side) and

`ServerSocket` (server side). This connection uses TCP/IP under the hood, which guarantees the message arrives intact and in order.

The Chat App Architecture

Here's the high-level design of our messaging system

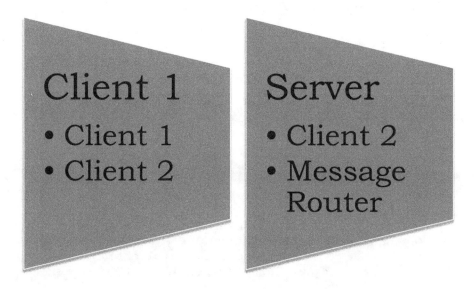

The server is responsible for listening on a port, accepting multiple connections (clients), and then routing messages between them. Each client connects using a socket, identifies itself with a nickname, and starts chatting.

8.3 Setting Up the Server

The server program uses a `ServerSocket` that listens for connections. Each new connection spawns a new thread to handle communication with that particular client.

Server Code Multi-Client Handling

```java
public class ChatServer {
    private static Set<ClientHandler> clientHandlers
= ConcurrentHashMap.newKeySet();

    public static void main(String[] args) {
        try (ServerSocket serverSocket = new
ServerSocket(9999)) {
            System.out.println("Chat server started
on port 9999...");
            while (true) {
                Socket clientSocket =
serverSocket.accept();
                ClientHandler client = new
ClientHandler(clientSocket);
                clientHandlers.add(client);
                new Thread(client).start();
            }
        } catch (IOException e) {
            e.printStackTrace();
        }
    }

    static void broadcast(String message,
ClientHandler sender) {
        for (ClientHandler client    clientHandlers) {
            if (client != sender) {
                client.sendMessage(message);
            }
```

```
        }
    }

    static void removeClient(ClientHandler client) {
        clientHandlers.remove(client);
    }
}
```

The `ChatServer` maintains a thread-safe set of all connected clients. When a new client joins, we spin up a `ClientHandler` thread to manage that individual's communication.

ClientHandler Class

```
class ClientHandler implements Runnable {
    private Socket socket;
    private PrintWriter out;
    private BufferedReader in;
    private String nickname;

    public ClientHandler(Socket socket) {
        this.socket = socket;
    }

    public void run() {
        try {
            out = new
PrintWriter(socket.getOutputStream(), true);
            in  = new BufferedReader(new
InputStreamReader(socket.getInputStream()));
            out.println("Enter your nickname ");
            nickname = in.readLine();
            ChatServer.broadcast(nickname + " joined
the chat.", this);

            String input;
            while ((input = in.readLine()) != null) {
```

```
                String time = "[" +
LocalTime.now().truncatedTo(ChronoUnit.SECONDS) +
"]";
                String fullMessage = time + " " +
nickname + "   " + input;
                ChatServer.broadcast(fullMessage,
this);
            }
        } catch (IOException e) {
            System.out.println("Connection error   " +
e.getMessage());
        } finally {
            ChatServer.removeClient(this);
            ChatServer.broadcast(nickname + " left
the chat.", this);
            try { socket.close(); } catch
(IOException ignored) {}
        }
    }

    public void sendMessage(String msg) {
        out.println(msg);
    }
}
```

Each connected client is managed in its own thread. This class handles nickname assignment, incoming message reading, and outgoing message sending.

8.4 Building the Client GUI

The client app provides a window for typing and reading messages. It must connect to the server via Socket, then handle incoming and outgoing streams in a separate thread to prevent the GUI from freezing.

GUI Layout Design

Let's plan the layout of the client interface

```
+-----------------------------------------------------
+
|              Local Network Chat Messenger
|
+-----------------------------------------------------
+
| Chat Log (JTextArea, non-editable, scrollable)
|
|
|
|
|
+-----------------------------------------------------
+
| [Nickname_____] [Connect]
|
| [Message_____] [Send]
|
+-----------------------------------------------------
+
```

We use JTextArea for displaying chat logs, JTextField for nickname and messages, and JButton for triggering connection and sending actions.

Client GUI Code

```java
public class ChatClient extends JFrame {
    private JTextArea chatArea;
    private JTextField messageField, nicknameField;
    private PrintWriter out;
    private Socket socket;

    public ChatClient() {
        setTitle("Java Chat Messenger");
        setSize(500, 400);
        setLayout(new BorderLayout());
```

```java
        setDefaultCloseOperation(EXIT_ON_CLOSE);

        chatArea = new JTextArea();
        chatArea.setEditable(false);
        JScrollPane scrollPane = new
JScrollPane(chatArea);

        messageField = new JTextField();
        JButton sendButton = new JButton("Send");

        nicknameField = new JTextField("Guest", 10);
        JButton connectButton = new
JButton("Connect");

        JPanel topPanel = new JPanel();
        topPanel.add(new JLabel("Nickname "));
        topPanel.add(nicknameField);
        topPanel.add(connectButton);

        JPanel bottomPanel = new JPanel(new
BorderLayout());
        bottomPanel.add(messageField,
BorderLayout.CENTER);
        bottomPanel.add(sendButton,
BorderLayout.EAST);

        add(topPanel, BorderLayout.NORTH);
        add(scrollPane, BorderLayout.CENTER);
        add(bottomPanel, BorderLayout.SOUTH);

        connectButton.addActionListener(e ->
connectToServer());
        sendButton.addActionListener(e ->
sendMessage());

        setVisible(true);
    }

    private void connectToServer() {
        try {
```

```java
            socket = new Socket("localhost", 9999);
            out = new
PrintWriter(socket.getOutputStream(), true);
            BufferedReader in = new
BufferedReader(new
InputStreamReader(socket.getInputStream()));

            new Thread(() -> {
                String line;
                try {
                    while ((line = in.readLine()) !=
null) {
                        chatArea.append(line + "\n");
                    }
                } catch (IOException e) {
                    e.printStackTrace();
                }
            }).start();

            out.println(nicknameField.getText());
        } catch (IOException e) {
            chatArea.append("Failed to connect to
server.\n");
        }
    }

    private void sendMessage() {
        if (out != null) {
            out.println(messageField.getText());
            messageField.setText("");
        }
    }

    public static void main(String[] args) {
        new ChatClient();
    }
}
```

This GUI allows users to enter a nickname, connect to the server, and begin sending and receiving messages with timestamps.

8.5 Logging Chat History to File

You can easily log the entire conversation to a file using `BufferedWriter` or `PrintWriter`.

For example, in the client thread

```
BufferedWriter logWriter = new BufferedWriter(new
FileWriter("chatlog.txt", true));
while ((line = in.readLine()) != null) {
    chatArea.append(line + "\n");
    logWriter.write(line + "\n");
    logWriter.flush();
}
```

This stores chat logs persistently for future reference, useful for audit or record keeping in enterprise chat tools.

8.6 Expanding the Project Ideas and Challenges

You now have a fully working local network chat tool. But this project is a playground for extending your creativity and technical prowess. You might consider adding

- Encrypted communication using SSL sockets for security

- Emoji support and message formatting with styled text panes
- File transfers between clients
- Notification popups for incoming messages using `SystemTray`
- Sound alerts for incoming messages

8.7 Key Concepts Learned

This chapter introduced real-world networking with Java, combining server and client roles, socket communication, multithreading for concurrent operations, Swing GUI programming, and chat history management. These are powerful concepts—understanding them can launch you into more advanced domains like game development, distributed systems, or online collaboration platforms.

A messaging app isn't just about typing and reading messages. It's about concurrency, communication, coordination, and user experience—all rolled into a single product. You've not only built a physical, usable product with Java in this chapter, but also leveled up your understanding of how network applications are born, structured, and made reliable. In the next chapter, we'll explore building a **media library manager**, where you'll handle files, metadata, search functionality, and previews. Stay curious, and keep building.

Chapter 9

Inventory Management System with Database (JDBC + SQLite)

Bridging the Gap Between Software and Persistent Data

In real-world applications, data rarely lives only in memory. From e-commerce platforms to warehouse control systems, the core of any meaningful desktop application involves interacting with structured, persistent data—usually stored in databases. This chapter introduces you to one of the most essential capabilities a desktop Java application must possess database integration. Using JDBC (Java Database Connectivity) and SQLite, we'll build a complete desktop inventory management system.

SQLite is the perfect companion for learning relational databases in desktop applications. It is serverless, zero-configuration, and stores its entire database in a single file. On the other hand, JDBC is Java's built-in API for interacting with relational databases, providing a universal mechanism to perform SQL queries, manage connections, and process results.

Together, SQLite and JDBC empower us to construct a fully functional inventory management system with persistent storage, real-time data access, form-driven interfaces, and even filtering and search functionalities.

Planning the Inventory System

An inventory system allows users to manage stock. For simplicity and focus, we will implement a single-table design that handles CRUD (Create, Read, Update, Delete) operations. Each product in our database will contain an ID, name, category, quantity, and price.

Step 1 Setting Up SQLite and JDBC Driver

Download the SQLite JDBC driver from https //github.com/xerial/sqlite-jdbc and add it to your project classpath. If using IntelliJ or Eclipse, include it as a library dependency.

Create the database manually or through code. Here's the Java code to initialize the database

```
public class DBHelper {
    private static final String DB_URL = "jdbc sqlite
inventory.db";

    public static Connection connect() throws
SQLException {
        return DriverManager.getConnection(DB_URL);
    }

    public static void initializeDB() {
        String sql = "CREATE TABLE IF NOT EXISTS
products ("
                + "id INTEGER PRIMARY KEY
AUTOINCREMENT,"
                + "name TEXT NOT NULL,"
                + "category TEXT NOT NULL,"
                + "quantity INTEGER,"
                + "price REAL");

        try (Connection conn = connect(); Statement
stmt = conn.createStatement()) {
            stmt.execute(sql);
        } catch (SQLException e) {
            e.printStackTrace();
        }
    }
}
```

Call `DBHelper.initializeDB();` in your application startup to ensure the table exists.

Step 2 Create the Product Model

Each product will be represented by a Java class

```
public class Product {
    private int id;
    private String name;
    private String category;
    private int quantity;
    private double price;

    // Constructors, Getters and Setters omitted for
brevity
}
```

This model helps us represent and transport data between the database and UI.

Step 3 Implementing CRUD Operations

We'll implement basic data access methods addProduct, updateProduct, deleteProduct, getAllProducts, and searchProductByName.

```
public class ProductDAO {
    public static void addProduct(Product p) throws
SQLException {
        String sql = "INSERT INTO products(name,
category, quantity, price) VALUES(?, ?, ?, ?)";
        try (Connection conn = DBHelper.connect();
PreparedStatement pstmt = conn.prepareStatement(sql))
{
            pstmt.setString(1, p.getName());
            pstmt.setString(2, p.getCategory());
            pstmt.setInt(3, p.getQuantity());
            pstmt.setDouble(4, p.getPrice());
            pstmt.executeUpdate();
```

```
            }
        }

    public static List<Product> getAllProducts()
throws SQLException {
            String sql = "SELECT * FROM products";
            List<Product> productList = new
ArrayList<>();
            try (Connection conn = DBHelper.connect();
Statement stmt = conn.createStatement(); ResultSet rs
= stmt.executeQuery(sql)) {
                while (rs.next()) {
                    Product p = new Product();
                    p.setId(rs.getInt("id"));
                    p.setName(rs.getString("name"));

p.setCategory(rs.getString("category"));
                    p.setQuantity(rs.getInt("quantity"));
                    p.setPrice(rs.getDouble("price"));
                    productList.add(p);
                }
            }
            return productList;
        }
}
```

You can similarly implement update and delete methods using
SQL UPDATE and DELETE queries with prepared statements.

Step 4 Designing the UI with Swing

Let's construct a form-based interface to add and display products
using Swing. Use JTable to show the list, JTextField for input,
and JButton for actions.

```
public class InventoryUI {
    private JFrame frame = new JFrame("Inventory
Management");
```

```java
    private JTable table;
    private DefaultTableModel model;
    private JTextField nameField = new
JTextField(15);
    private JTextField categoryField = new
JTextField(15);
    private JTextField quantityField = new
JTextField(5);
    private JTextField priceField = new
JTextField(7);
    private JButton addButton = new JButton("Add
Product");

    public InventoryUI() {
        frame.setSize(800, 500);
        frame.setLayout(new BorderLayout());
        model = new DefaultTableModel(new
String[]{"ID", "Name", "Category", "Qty", "Price"},
0);
        table = new JTable(model);
        JScrollPane scrollPane = new
JScrollPane(table);
        frame.add(scrollPane, BorderLayout.CENTER);

        JPanel formPanel = new JPanel();
        formPanel.add(new JLabel("Name "));
        formPanel.add(nameField);
        formPanel.add(new JLabel("Category "));
        formPanel.add(categoryField);
        formPanel.add(new JLabel("Qty "));
        formPanel.add(quantityField);
        formPanel.add(new JLabel("Price "));
        formPanel.add(priceField);
        formPanel.add(addButton);

        frame.add(formPanel, BorderLayout.SOUTH);

frame.setDefaultCloseOperation(JFrame.EXIT_ON_CLOSE);
        frame.setVisible(true);
```

```java
        addButton.addActionListener(e ->
addProduct());
        loadProducts();
    }

    private void addProduct() {
        try {
            Product p = new Product();
            p.setName(nameField.getText());
            p.setCategory(categoryField.getText());

p.setQuantity(Integer.parseInt(quantityField.getText(
)));

p.setPrice(Double.parseDouble(priceField.getText()));
            ProductDAO.addProduct(p);
            loadProducts();
        } catch (Exception ex) {
            JOptionPane.showMessageDialog(frame,
"Error  " + ex.getMessage());
        }
    }

    private void loadProducts() {
        try {
            model.setRowCount(0);
            for (Product p
ProductDAO.getAllProducts()) {
                model.addRow(new Object[]{p.getId(),
p.getName(), p.getCategory(), p.getQuantity(),
p.getPrice()});
            }
        } catch (SQLException ex) {
            ex.printStackTrace();
        }
    }

    public static void main(String[] args) {
        DBHelper.initializeDB();
        new InventoryUI();
```

```
    }
}
```

Visualization The Component Layout

```
+--------------------------------+
|          JTable Display        |
|--------------------------------|
|  ID | Name | Qty | Price       |
+--------------------------------+
| Form Inputs and Add Button     |
|   Name | Category | Qty | $     |
|      [Add Product Button]       |
+--------------------------------+
```

What This Project Teaches You

By completing this project, readers will deeply understand how desktop applications communicate with relational databases using SQL. Skills acquired include designing schemas, implementing persistence with JDBC, managing exceptions, building interactive Swing interfaces, and creating user-friendly forms that manipulate backend data. These skills are applicable in countless software development roles and serve as a bridge toward enterprise software development, Android SQLite usage, and JDBC-backed web applications.

This chapter transforms abstract database theory into a tangible, functional application. By building an inventory system from the ground up, readers will master the flow of persistent data from GUI to disk and back—an essential milestone in becoming a skilled Java developer.

Chapter 10

Image Viewer & Editor

In today's digital world, image viewing and editing are essential features for many desktop applications. The ability to manipulate images—whether to apply filters, crop, resize, or rotate them—enhances user experience in a wide variety of programs. In this chapter, we will design and implement a basic photo viewer and editor using Java Swing and Java 2D API. Along the way, we will cover key concepts like loading images, manipulating pixel data, and implementing common image processing features such as zoom, rotate, grayscale filters, and batch renaming.

This project is not just about displaying images, but also providing hands-on experience with image manipulation and graphical user interfaces (GUIs). After completing this chapter, you will be equipped with the knowledge to extend the application with additional features, potentially turning it into a fully functional image editor.

Setting Up the Project

Before diving into the implementation, let's ensure we have a proper development environment set up. To build this image viewer and editor, you will need

JDK (Java Development Kit) – Ensure you have JDK installed (version 8 or higher).

IDE – We recommend using an IDE like IntelliJ IDEA or Eclipse for this project.

Swing Library – This is already included in the JDK, so there's no need for external libraries.

Java 2D API – Java's 2D API, which is part of the Java SE library, provides tools for image manipulation and rendering graphics.

Step 1 Designing the GUI

We will design a simple Swing-based interface with components to load an image, view it, zoom in and out, rotate it, and apply basic filters. The core components of the application will include

JFrame for the main window.

JMenuBar for the menu options like file operations and image processing options.

JPanel for displaying the image.

JButtons for user interaction such as zooming and rotating the image.

JLabel to show the image.

We'll begin by setting up the basic components of the GUI.

```java
import javax.swing.*;
import java.awt.*;
import java.awt.event.*;
import java.io.*;
import javax.imageio.*;
import java.awt.image.*;

public class ImageEditorUI {
    private JFrame frame;
    private JLabel imageLabel;
    private BufferedImage image;
    private File imageFile;
    private String imagePath = "";

    public ImageEditorUI() {
        frame = new JFrame("Image Viewer & Editor");

frame.setDefaultCloseOperation(JFrame.EXIT_ON_CLOSE);
        frame.setSize(800, 600);
        frame.setLayout(new BorderLayout());

        // Image display panel
        imageLabel = new JLabel();
        frame.add(imageLabel, BorderLayout.CENTER);

        // Menu bar
        JMenuBar menuBar = new JMenuBar();
        JMenu fileMenu = new JMenu("File");
        JMenuItem openItem = new JMenuItem("Open");
        openItem.addActionListener(e -> openImage());
        fileMenu.add(openItem);
        menuBar.add(fileMenu);
        frame.setJMenuBar(menuBar);

        // Tool buttons
        JPanel buttonPanel = new JPanel();
        JButton zoomInButton = new JButton("Zoom
In");
        zoomInButton.addActionListener(e ->
zoomImage(1.2));
```

```java
        JButton zoomOutButton = new JButton("Zoom
Out");
        zoomOutButton.addActionListener(e ->
zoomImage(0.8));
        JButton rotateButton = new JButton("Rotate");
        rotateButton.addActionListener(e ->
rotateImage());
        JButton grayscaleButton = new
JButton("Grayscale");
        grayscaleButton.addActionListener(e ->
applyGrayscale());

        buttonPanel.add(zoomInButton);
        buttonPanel.add(zoomOutButton);
        buttonPanel.add(rotateButton);
        buttonPanel.add(grayscaleButton);

        frame.add(buttonPanel, BorderLayout.SOUTH);

        frame.setVisible(true);
    }

    private void openImage() {
        JFileChooser fileChooser = new
JFileChooser();
        int returnValue =
fileChooser.showOpenDialog(frame);
        if (returnValue ==
JFileChooser.APPROVE_OPTION) {
            imagePath =
fileChooser.getSelectedFile().getAbsolutePath();
            try {
                image = ImageIO.read(new
File(imagePath));
                ImageIcon icon = new
ImageIcon(image);
                imageLabel.setIcon(icon);
                frame.repaint();
            } catch (IOException e) {
```

```java
                JOptionPane.showMessageDialog(frame,
"Error opening image.");
            }
        }
    }

    private void zoomImage(double scaleFactor) {
        if (image != null) {
            int width = (int) (image.getWidth() *
scaleFactor);
            int height = (int) (image.getHeight() *
scaleFactor);
            Image scaledImage =
image.getScaledInstance(width, height,
Image.SCALE_SMOOTH);
            image = new BufferedImage(width, height,
BufferedImage.TYPE_INT_ARGB);
            Graphics g = image.getGraphics();
            g.drawImage(scaledImage, 0, 0, null);
            imageLabel.setIcon(new ImageIcon(image));
        }
    }

    private void rotateImage() {
        if (image != null) {
            int width = image.getWidth();
            int height = image.getHeight();
            BufferedImage rotatedImage = new
BufferedImage(height, width, image.getType());
            Graphics2D g2d =
rotatedImage.createGraphics();
            g2d.rotate(Math.toRadians(90), width / 2,
height / 2);
            g2d.drawImage(image, 0, 0, null);
            g2d.dispose();
            image = rotatedImage;
            imageLabel.setIcon(new ImageIcon(image));
        }
    }
```

```java
    private void applyGrayscale() {
        if (image != null) {
            for (int i = 0; i < image.getWidth();
i++) {
                for (int j = 0; j <
image.getHeight(); j++) {
                    Color color = new
Color(image.getRGB(i, j));
                    int red = color.getRed();
                    int green = color.getGreen();
                    int blue = color.getBlue();
                    int gray = (int) (red * 0.3 +
green * 0.59 + blue * 0.11);
                    Color grayColor = new Color(gray,
gray, gray);
                    image.setRGB(i, j,
grayColor.getRGB());
                }
            }
            imageLabel.setIcon(new ImageIcon(image));
        }
    }

    public static void main(String[] args) {
        SwingUtilities.invokeLater(ImageEditorUI
new);
    }
}
```

Step 2 Zooming the Image

Zooming is accomplished by scaling the image up or
down using the getScaledInstance method. This
method resizes the image based on a scale factor. For
example, if the user clicks "Zoom In", we increase the
image size by 1.2 times its original dimensions.

When the zoom operation is triggered, the image is re-rendered in its new size. The `zoomImage()` method resizes the image and updates the display, ensuring a smooth user experience.

Step 3 Rotating the Image

The rotation operation is performed using the `Graphics2D` class, which allows for a rotation transformation. We rotate the image by 90 degrees around its center. The image is first drawn to a new `BufferedImage` with its width and height swapped, and then the rotated image is displayed.

The `rotateImage()` method rotates the image by 90 degrees, which is a typical rotation increment. However, this can be modified to allow for more flexible rotation (e.g., user-defined angles).

Step 4 Applying Grayscale Filter

The grayscale filter converts each pixel to a shade of gray based on its red, green, and blue (RGB) components. The formula used is

```
Gray = (0.3 * Red) + (0.59 * Green) + (0.11 * Blue)
```

This is a standard approach to creating grayscale images, where the red, green, and blue channels are weighted based on human perception of light.

In the `applyGrayscale()` method, the image is iterated pixel by pixel, and the RGB values are converted to grayscale. The updated image is then displayed.

Step 5 Batch Renaming Feature (Optional)

For batch renaming, the user can select multiple images and apply a consistent naming scheme (e.g., "image1.jpg", "image2.jpg"). This can be achieved by looping through selected files and renaming them using `File.renameTo()`.

By completing this project, you gained hands-on experience with Java's image processing capabilities through the 2D API. You learned how to

- Load and display images using Swing.
- Implement zoom, rotation, and grayscale filters.
- Manipulate pixel data directly.
- Build an interactive user interface for image editing.

You now have the foundation to explore more advanced image processing techniques such as cropping, applying custom filters, or even integrating third-party libraries for more complex tasks.

This chapter provides a comprehensive, practical introduction to Java image manipulation, and serves as a great springboard for more complex image editing applications.

Chapter 11

PDF Report Generator App

In today's digital world, reports are a fundamental part of various industries. Whether you're generating business reports, invoices, or even research papers, having a reliable and efficient way to create and manage PDF documents is a crucial skill for any developer. This chapter will guide you through building a simple yet powerful PDF report generator using Java. By the end of this chapter, you will have a solid understanding of how to dynamically generate PDF reports based on user input and data, as well as how to incorporate file dialogs for better user experience.

We will use a popular Java library called **iText** (or **Apache PDFBox** as an alternative) to handle PDF creation. These libraries are widely used for generating and manipulating PDF files in Java, and they offer a wide range of features, from adding images and tables to embedding hyperlinks and text formatting.

The goal of this chapter is not just to build a functional PDF report generator but also to teach you the essentials of file manipulation, dynamic document creation, and integrating file dialogs into your Java Swing applications. Along the way, you will gain a deeper understanding of handling various types of data input and generating reports that can be easily shared, printed, or saved.

Step 1 Setting Up the Development Environment

Before we start building the application, let's ensure that our development environment is properly configured. The first thing we need is to install the required library for handling PDF generation. We will use **iText** for this project, but **Apache PDFBox** is a good alternative if you prefer it.

Installing iText

To use **iText** in your project, you can include it using Maven. If you're using a build tool like Maven or Gradle, the easiest way is to add the following dependency to your project's configuration.

Maven

```
<dependency>
    <groupId>com.itextpdf</groupId>
    <artifactId>itext7-core</artifactId>
    <version>7.2.4</version>
</dependency>
```

Alternatively, if you prefer to manually download and include the jar files, you can download iText from the official website and include the JAR in your project's classpath.

Once you've set up iText in your project, you're ready to start working on the PDF report generator.

Step 2 Designing the User Interface

The user interface (UI) for our report generator will be quite simple. It needs to allow the user to input some data, such as a report title, author, content, and date. Based on this input, the program will dynamically generate a PDF report.

Our application will contain the following components

JTextField For entering the report title and author.

JTextArea For entering the content of the report.

JButton To generate and save the PDF report.

JFileChooser To allow the user to choose the location to save the generated PDF report.

Below is a simple layout for the application

```
-----------------------------------------------------
|                PDF Report Generator               |
|---------------------------------------------------|
| Title  [                        ]                 |
| Author [                        ]                 |
|---------------------------------------------------|
| Report Content                                    |
| [                                            ]    |
|                                                   |
| [                                            ]    |
|                                                   |
|---------------------------------------------------|
| [Generate PDF] [Browse for Save Location]         |
-----------------------------------------------------
```

The user will input a title, author, and content into the appropriate text fields. Once the data is entered, the user can click the **Generate PDF** button, which will generate a PDF report with the provided information.

Step 3 Writing the Code for PDF Generation

The core functionality of this application is the PDF report generation. We will use **iText** to create the PDF document. To generate a simple PDF, we will follow these steps

Create a Document object The document is the container for the content of our PDF.

Create a PdfWriter object This writer is used to write the content to the actual PDF file.

Add content to the document Using iText's `Paragraph` and other elements, we will add the report's title, author, content, and date.

Save the document to a file Once the content is added, we will save the document to the desired location.

Here is a basic implementation of generating a PDF report using iText

```
import com.itextpdf.text.*;
import com.itextpdf.text.pdf.*;
```

```java
import javax.swing.*;
import java.io.File;
import java.io.FileOutputStream;
import java.io.IOException;

public class PDFReportGenerator {

    private JTextField titleField;
    private JTextField authorField;
    private JTextArea contentArea;

    public PDFReportGenerator() {
        // Create the UI components
        JFrame frame = new JFrame("PDF Report
Generator");

frame.setDefaultCloseOperation(JFrame.EXIT_ON_CLOSE);
        frame.setSize(400, 300);
        frame.setLayout(new
BoxLayout(frame.getContentPane(), BoxLayout.Y_AXIS));

        // Title input
        JPanel titlePanel = new JPanel();
        titlePanel.add(new JLabel("Title "));
        titleField = new JTextField(20);
        titlePanel.add(titleField);
        frame.add(titlePanel);

        // Author input
        JPanel authorPanel = new JPanel();
        authorPanel.add(new JLabel("Author "));
        authorField = new JTextField(20);
        authorPanel.add(authorField);
        frame.add(authorPanel);

        // Report content input
        JPanel contentPanel = new JPanel();
        contentPanel.add(new JLabel("Report Content
"));
```

```java
        contentArea = new JTextArea(10, 30);
        JScrollPane scrollPane = new
JScrollPane(contentArea);
        contentPanel.add(scrollPane);
        frame.add(contentPanel);

        // Generate PDF button
        JButton generateButton = new
JButton("Generate PDF");
        generateButton.addActionListener(e ->
generatePDF());
        frame.add(generateButton);

        // Set frame visible
        frame.setVisible(true);
    }

    private void generatePDF() {
        // Retrieve user input
        String title = titleField.getText();
        String author = authorField.getText();
        String content = contentArea.getText();

        // Define the file path to save the PDF
        JFileChooser fileChooser = new
JFileChooser();
        fileChooser.setDialogTitle("Save PDF");
        int result =
fileChooser.showSaveDialog(null);

        if (result == JFileChooser.APPROVE_OPTION) {
            File file =
fileChooser.getSelectedFile();

            try {
                // Create the PDF document
                Document document = new Document();
                PdfWriter.getInstance(document, new
FileOutputStream(file));
                document.open();
```

```java
                    // Add title, author, and content to
the PDF
                    Paragraph titlePara = new
Paragraph(title,
FontFactory.getFont(FontFactory.HELVETICA_BOLD, 18));

titlePara.setAlignment(Element.ALIGN_CENTER);
                    document.add(titlePara);

                    Paragraph authorPara = new
Paragraph("By  " + author,
FontFactory.getFont(FontFactory.HELVETICA, 12));

authorPara.setAlignment(Element.ALIGN_CENTER);
                    document.add(authorPara);

                    document.add(new Paragraph(" "));
                    document.add(new Paragraph(content));

                    // Close the document
                    document.close();

                    JOptionPane.showMessageDialog(null,
"PDF Generated Successfully!");
            } catch (DocumentException | IOException
ex) {
                    JOptionPane.showMessageDialog(null,
"Error generating PDF  " + ex.getMessage());
            }
        }
    }

    public static void main(String[] args) {
        SwingUtilities.invokeLater(PDFReportGenerator
new);
    }
}
```

In this code, the `generatePDF` method retrieves the title, author, and content entered by the user. It then uses the **iText** library to create a new PDF document. The `PdfWriter` writes the content to a file that the user chooses using a `JFileChooser` dialog. The document is formatted with a title, author, and content, and then saved to the specified file.

The `JFileChooser` allows the user to choose where to save the generated PDF file, and the PDF is then written to disk using **iText**'s `Document` and `PdfWriter` classes. The result is a simple but dynamic PDF report that can be opened, printed, or shared.

Step 4 Customizing the Report Layout

While the basic PDF report works, you may want to improve the layout by adding features like headers, footers, tables, and styling. iText allows you to easily add all these elements to your report.

For example, you can add tables to your reports using iText's `PdfPTable` class. Here's a quick example of adding a table to your PDF

```
PdfPTable table = new PdfPTable(3); // 3 columns
table.addCell("Column 1");
table.addCell("Column 2");
table.addCell("Column 3");

// Add rows to the table
```

117

```
table.addCell("Data 1");
table.addCell("Data 2");
table.addCell("Data 3");

document.add(table);
```

Similarly, you can apply custom fonts, set text alignment, and add images to your PDF report using the methods provided by iText.

In this chapter, we have learned how to build a simple PDF report generator application using Java Swing and the iText library. We explored the basics of generating PDF files, handling user input, and saving the generated document to the user's chosen location.

Along the way, we introduced key concepts like document creation, file handling, and integrating file dialogs into desktop applications. We also explored how to enhance the layout and design of the report by adding tables and customizing fonts and styles.

This project is a great starting point for anyone interested in generating professional-looking reports, invoices, or any other type of printable document from Java applications. With this knowledge, you can extend the application by adding more complex features like report templates, data-driven content, and automatic PDF generation based on external data sources.

Chapter 12

Desktop Weather Dashboard Using Web APIs

In this chapter, we are going to build a **Weather Dashboard** application using Java. This project will involve fetching real-time weather data from a public API, specifically **OpenWeatherMap**, parsing that data, and displaying it on a graphical user interface (GUI). Not only will this help you understand how to consume web APIs in Java, but it will also teach you important skills such as parsing JSON, making HTTP requests, and working with external data to create dynamic, real-time applications.

Step 1 Understanding the Project

The goal of this project is to create a desktop weather dashboard where the user can enter a location (city or zip code) and get current weather data such as temperature, humidity, weather description, and wind speed. This data will be fetched from the **OpenWeatherMap API**, which provides weather data in JSON format. After retrieving the data, we will parse it and display it in a structured way within a **Java Swing** GUI.

The steps to implement this project include

Setting up the environment by integrating the necessary libraries for making HTTP requests.

Fetching weather data from OpenWeatherMap using a GET request.

Parsing JSON data and extracting the relevant weather information.

Building a GUI that displays the weather data in an organized and visually appealing way.

Handling errors such as invalid city names or failed API requests gracefully.

By the end of this chapter, you'll have a functional weather dashboard and a solid understanding of how to build applications that interact with web APIs.

Step 2 Setting Up the Project Environment

To get started, ensure you have the following setup

Java Development Kit (JDK) Make sure you have JDK installed and configured on your system. This tutorial uses JDK 8 or higher.

IDE We recommend using an Integrated Development Environment (IDE) like IntelliJ IDEA or Eclipse to streamline development.

Libraries We will use the **HttpURLConnection** class for making HTTP requests and **org.json** (or **Gson/ Jackson**) for parsing JSON. You will need to include a

JSON library in your project. If you're using Maven, you can add the dependency for **org.json** like this

```
<dependency>
    <groupId>org.json</groupId>
    <artifactId>json</artifactId>
    <version>20210307</version>
</dependency>
```

If you're not using Maven, you can download the **json.jar** file and include it in your project's classpath.

API Key for OpenWeatherMap To interact with the OpenWeatherMap API, you will need to sign up for a free account and get an API key. This key is required to make requests to the API.

Step 3   Fetching Weather Data Using the OpenWeatherMap API

To fetch weather data, we will make an HTTP **GET** request to the **OpenWeatherMap API**. The URL for the API request is structured like this

```
http
//api.openweathermap.org/data/2.5/weather?q={CITY_NAME}&appid={API_KEY}
```

Where {CITY_NAME} is the name of the city you want the weather data for, and {API_KEY} is the API key that you obtained earlier.

We will use **HttpURLConnection** to send the request and receive the response. Below is a sample code to fetch weather data from OpenWeatherMap

```java
import java.io.BufferedReader;
import java.io.InputStreamReader;
import java.net.HttpURLConnection;
import java.net.URL;

public class WeatherAPI {

    public static String getWeatherData(String city)
throws Exception {
        String apiKey = "your_api_key_here"; //
Replace with your OpenWeatherMap API key
        String urlString = "http
//api.openweathermap.org/data/2.5/weather?q=" + city
+ "&appid=" + apiKey;

        // Create URL object
        URL url = new URL(urlString);

        // Create connection
        HttpURLConnection connection =
(HttpURLConnection) url.openConnection();
        connection.setRequestMethod("GET");

        // Read the response
        BufferedReader in = new BufferedReader(new
InputStreamReader(connection.getInputStream()));
        String inputLine;
        StringBuilder response = new StringBuilder();

        while ((inputLine = in.readLine()) != null) {
            response.append(inputLine);
        }
        in.close();
```

```
        return response.toString(); // Return JSON
response as a string
    }
}
```

In this code, the **getWeatherData** method constructs
the URL using the city name and your API key, sends
the GET request, and then reads the response into a
string. The response is a JSON string that contains all
the weather data for the specified city.

Step 4 Parsing the JSON Data

Once we have received the JSON response, we need to
parse it to extract relevant weather information such
as temperature, humidity, and weather description.
We will use the **org.json** library to parse the JSON
data.

Below is the code that parses the JSON response

```
import org.json.JSONObject;

public class WeatherParser {

    public static void parseWeatherData(String
jsonResponse) {
        // Parse JSON response
        JSONObject jsonObject = new
JSONObject(jsonResponse);

        // Extract weather details
        String cityName =
jsonObject.getString("name");
```

```java
        JSONObject main =
jsonObject.getJSONObject("main");
        double temperature = main.getDouble("temp") -
273.15; // Convert from Kelvin to Celsius
        int humidity = main.getInt("humidity");
        String weatherDescription =
jsonObject.getJSONArray("weather").getJSONObject(0).g
etString("description");
        JSONObject wind =
jsonObject.getJSONObject("wind");
        double windSpeed = wind.getDouble("speed");

        // Display weather information
        System.out.println("Weather in " + cityName +
" ");
        System.out.println("Temperature   " +
String.format("%.2f", temperature) + " °C");
        System.out.println("Humidity   " + humidity +
" %");
        System.out.println("Description   " +
weatherDescription);
        System.out.println("Wind Speed   " + windSpeed
+ " m/s");
    }
}
```

In this code, we extract

City Name from the `name` field.

Temperature from the `main` object and convert it from Kelvin to Celsius.

Humidity from the `main` object.

Weather Description from the `weather` array (the description is in the first element of the array).

Wind Speed from the `wind` object.

We then display this information in a user-friendly way.

Step 5 Building the User Interface (GUI)

Now that we have all the necessary data, we will build a simple **Java Swing** interface to display the weather information. The interface will consist of a text field for the user to input the city name, a button to fetch the weather data, and labels to display the weather details.

Here's the code to create the basic layout

```java
import javax.swing.*;
import java.awt.*;
import java.awt.event.ActionEvent;
import java.awt.event.ActionListener;

public class WeatherDashboard {

    private JFrame frame;
    private JTextField cityInput;
    private JLabel tempLabel;
    private JLabel humidityLabel;
    private JLabel descriptionLabel;
    private JLabel windSpeedLabel;

    public WeatherDashboard() {
        frame = new JFrame("Weather Dashboard");

frame.setDefaultCloseOperation(JFrame.EXIT_ON_CLOSE);
        frame.setSize(400, 300);
```

```java
        frame.setLayout(new FlowLayout());

        // City input
        cityInput = new JTextField(20);
        frame.add(cityInput);

        // Fetch Weather Button
        JButton fetchButton = new JButton("Fetch
Weather");
        frame.add(fetchButton);

        // Weather Info Labels
        tempLabel = new JLabel("Temperature  ");
        frame.add(tempLabel);
        humidityLabel = new JLabel("Humidity  ");
        frame.add(humidityLabel);
        descriptionLabel = new JLabel("Description
");
        frame.add(descriptionLabel);
        windSpeedLabel = new JLabel("Wind Speed  ");
        frame.add(windSpeedLabel);

        // Action listener for the button
        fetchButton.addActionListener(new
ActionListener() {
            @Override
            public void actionPerformed(ActionEvent
e) {
                String city = cityInput.getText();
                try {
                    String jsonResponse =
WeatherAPI.getWeatherData(city);

WeatherParser.parseWeatherData(jsonResponse);
                } catch (Exception ex) {

JOptionPane.showMessageDialog(frame, "Error fetching
data", "Error", JOptionPane.ERROR_MESSAGE);
                }
            }
```

```
        });

        frame.setVisible(true);
    }

    public static void main(String[] args) {
        SwingUtilities.invokeLater(() -> new
WeatherDashboard());
    }
}
```

In this code

- The **JTextField** is used for the user to input the city name.
- The **JButton** triggers the action of fetching the weather.
- The **JLabels** are used to display the weather information.
- The button's `ActionListener` fetches the weather data by calling the `WeatherAPI.getWeatherData` method and then parses the response using the `WeatherParser.parseWeatherData` method.

Step 6 Error Handling and User Experience

As with any application that involves external APIs, it's essential to handle errors gracefully. The weather API may return errors for invalid city names or network issues. In the `ActionListener`, we wrap the API request in a `try-catch` block to handle any exceptions. If an error occurs, a dialog box will pop up informing the user.

Additionally, you can enhance the user experience by

- Adding loading indicators while waiting for the API response.
- Showing more detailed weather information such as pressure, sunrise/sunset times, etc.
- Using images or icons to visually represent the weather conditions (e.g., clouds, sun, rain).

By following this chapter, you have learned how to build a **desktop weather dashboard** using **Java Swing** and an external **web API**. This project introduced you to making HTTP requests, parsing JSON data, and dynamically updating the GUI based on real-time data. Not only have you learned how to interact with APIs, but you've also gained valuable experience in handling real-world challenges like data parsing, error handling, and designing user-friendly interfaces.

This skill is highly valuable in today's world where external data is commonly used in desktop applications, and it serves as a foundation for building more complex, data-driven apps. You can further enhance this app by adding features like weather forecasts, multiple cities, or a graph to represent the weather data over time.

Chapter 13

Java-Based File Organizer Tool

In this chapter, we will be building a **Java-based file organizer tool**, designed to help users automate the process of sorting files within directories. This tool will categorize files based on different attributes such as file type, size, or the date the file was created. By using Java's built-in file management capabilities, along with a simple graphical user interface (GUI) to facilitate interaction, users will learn how to develop a practical and useful desktop tool. This chapter also introduces essential concepts in file traversal, working with file metadata, and implementing drag-and-drop functionality.

Understanding the Project

This project will allow users to choose a directory, scan the files within it, and then automatically organize them into subfolders based on certain criteria such as file type, size, or creation/modification date. For example, all image files can be moved into a folder labeled "Images," all document files into a folder labeled "Documents," and so on. Additionally, users will be able to sort files into directories based on their sizes (e.g., files smaller than 1MB in one folder, larger than 1MB in another), or based on the date they were last modified.

To achieve this, we will need to work with Java's **File class**, handle directories, perform metadata extraction, and create a user-friendly interface for users to interact with.

By the end of this chapter, you will have a fully functional file organizer that can be easily customized and extended to meet more specific needs, such as supporting more advanced file sorting algorithms, integrating with cloud storage, or adding additional filters and actions based on metadata.

Step 1 Setting Up the Development Environment

Before we dive into the project, ensure you have the following setup

Java Development Kit (JDK) Install the latest version of JDK (JDK 8 or later). This tutorial is compatible with most versions.

IDE A good Integrated Development Environment (IDE) like IntelliJ IDEA, Eclipse, or NetBeans is highly recommended.

Libraries For this project, Java's **Swing** for the graphical interface and **java.nio.file** for file handling will be our primary libraries. These come with the standard Java installation, so no additional libraries are required.

Step 2 Basic File Traversal

To start, we need to traverse a given directory and retrieve the files within it. Java provides the `java.nio.file` package, which contains the `Files` class and the `Paths` class, which will help us efficiently navigate the file system.

Here is a simple method to list all the files within a given directory

```
import java.io.File;
import java.nio.file.*;

public class FileOrganizer {

    public static void listFilesInDirectory(String
directoryPath) {
        Path path = Paths.get(directoryPath);
        try {
            Files.walk(path)  // Traverse the
directory tree
                    .filter(Files  isRegularFile)  //
Only regular files
                    .forEach(file ->
System.out.println(file));
        } catch (IOException e) {
            System.out.println("Error reading the
directory  " + e.getMessage());
        }
    }
}
```

In this example, we use `Files.walk()` to traverse the directory tree, and the `filter()` method ensures that only files (not directories) are listed. Each file is then printed to the console. This gives us a list of files that we can manipulate further.

The `walk()` method is ideal for traversing directories recursively, which means that all nested directories will also be explored.

Step 3 Extracting File Metadata

Once we have a list of files, the next step is to extract important metadata, such as file size, type, and modification date. For this, Java provides the `File` class, which offers a variety of methods to retrieve such information.

The following example demonstrates how to extract file metadata, such as the size and last modified date

```java
import java.io.File;

public class FileMetadata {

    public static void printFileMetadata(String
filePath) {
        File file = new File(filePath);

        if (file.exists()) {
            System.out.println("File Name   " +
file.getName());
            System.out.println("File Size   " +
file.length() + " bytes");
```

```
        System.out.println("Last Modified  " +
new java.util.Date(file.lastModified()));
        } else {
            System.out.println("The file does not
exist.");
        }
    }
}
```

Here, the `length()` method returns the size of the file in bytes, and `lastModified()` provides the timestamp of when the file was last modified.

To extract the file type, we can use the file's extension, which is easily obtained by calling the `getName()` method and then extracting the substring after the last period (.) to identify the file type.

This will help us categorize the files based on their type, size, or date.

Step 4 Organizing Files by Type, Size, or Date

Now, we'll implement the core functionality of our file organizer sorting files by type, size, and modification date.

To organize files by type, we will check the file extension and group files accordingly. Here's how we can do this

```
import java.io.File;
```

```java
import java.nio.file.*;
import java.util.*;

public class FileOrganizer {

    public static void organizeFilesByType(String
directoryPath) {
        Path path = Paths.get(directoryPath);
        Map<String, List<File>> fileMap = new
HashMap<>();

        try {
            Files.walk(path)
                .filter(Files  isRegularFile)
                .forEach(file -> {
                    String extension =
getFileExtension(file.toFile());
                    fileMap.putIfAbsent(extension,
new ArrayList<>());

fileMap.get(extension).add(file.toFile());
                });

            fileMap.forEach((extension, files) -> {
                System.out.println("Files of type " +
extension + " ");
                files.forEach(f ->
System.out.println(f.getName()));
            });

        } catch (IOException e) {
            System.out.println("Error reading the
directory  " + e.getMessage());
        }
    }

    private static String getFileExtension(File file)
{
        String fileName = file.getName();
        int dotIndex = fileName.lastIndexOf(".");
```

```
        if (dotIndex != -1) {
            return fileName.substring(dotIndex + 1);
        }
        return "unknown";
    }
}
```

In this code

We use `Files.walk()` to traverse the directory and retrieve all regular files.

For each file, we extract its file extension using the helper method `getFileExtension()`.

We store files in a `Map<String, List<File>>`, where the key is the file extension and the value is a list of files of that type.

After grouping the files, we print out the files for each type.

This can be extended further by organizing the files into directories corresponding to their file types, making the sorting process more visual.

Step 5 Drag-and-Drop Functionality

To make the tool more user-friendly, we can add **drag-and-drop functionality** to allow users to simply drag a folder or file into the application window for sorting.

This can be achieved using the **Java Swing** library, which provides support for drag-and-drop operations.

Here's how we can implement drag-and-drop support in a JFrame

```java
import javax.swing.*;
import java.awt.*;
import java.awt.dnd.*;
import java.io.File;

public class DragDropOrganizer extends JFrame {

    public DragDropOrganizer() {
        setTitle("Drag and Drop File Organizer");
        setSize(400, 300);

setDefaultCloseOperation(JFrame.EXIT_ON_CLOSE);
        setLocationRelativeTo(null);

        // Enable drag-and-drop
        new DropTarget(this,
DnDConstants.ACTION_COPY, new FileDropListener(),
true);

        setVisible(true);
    }

    private class FileDropListener implements
DropTargetListener {

        @Override
        public void dragEnter(DropTargetDragEvent
dtde) {}

        @Override
        public void dragOver(DropTargetDragEvent
dtde) {}
```

```java
        @Override
        public void drop(DropTargetDropEvent dtde) {
            try {

dtde.acceptDrop(DnDConstants.ACTION_COPY);
                java.util.List<File> droppedFiles =
(java.util.List<File>)
dtde.getTransferable().getTransferData(DataFlavor.jav
aFileListFlavor);
                droppedFiles.forEach(file ->
System.out.println("Dropped  " +
file.getAbsolutePath()));
            } catch (Exception e) {
                e.printStackTrace();
            }
        }

        @Override
        public void dragExit(DropTargetEvent dte) {}

        @Override
        public void
dropActionChanged(DropTargetDragEvent dtde) {}
    }

    public static void main(String[] args) {
        new DragDropOrganizer();
    }
}
```

In this code, we use the DropTarget class to add drag-and-drop functionality to the JFrame. When files or directories are dropped onto the window, they are processed and the path is printed.

You can modify this example to trigger the file sorting process when a directory is dropped onto the window.

Step 6 Finalizing the Application

At this point, you have the essential components of the **File Organizer Tool**

1. The ability to traverse and list files in a directory.
2. The capability to sort files by type, size, or modification date.
3. Drag-and-drop functionality to enhance the user experience.

To finalize the application, you can extend it with features such as

File renaming Allow users to rename files based on certain patterns or batch rename files.

File search Implement a search functionality to allow users to find specific files by name or type.

User preferences Allow users to save sorting preferences, such as default file type categories or size thresholds.

In this chapter, you learned how to build a **Java-based file organizer tool** from the ground up. By using Java's file-handling capabilities, we were able to create a tool that sorts files based on their attributes, helping users keep their file systems organized. You were introduced to concepts such as file traversal, metadata extraction, drag-and-drop functionality, and working with Java Swing for the user interface.

Chapter 14

Build a Desktop Quiz App with Scoring System

In this chapter, we will guide you through the process of building a **Desktop Quiz Application** using Java. The primary focus of this project is to design a quiz app that loads questions from an external file (in XML or JSON format), tracks the user's progress, and displays scores at the end of the quiz. By working through this project, you will learn how to handle file parsing, model data as objects, and design an interactive graphical user interface (GUI). This quiz app will serve as a fun yet practical project, reinforcing your Java skills while giving you a hands-on experience in creating a user-driven application.

Understanding the Project Requirements

The **quiz app** will be a simple but interactive application that

Loads Questions from a File The questions and their corresponding answers will be stored in an external file (XML or JSON). The app will read the file, extract the data, and use it to generate the quiz.

Tracks Progress The app will keep track of which question the user is on and store their answers.

Scoring System As the user answers questions, the app will calculate a score based on correct responses.

Interactive User Interface (UI) The interface will be built using Java Swing, providing a simple but interactive platform for users to take the quiz.

By building this app, you will learn how to work with external data formats, manage application state, and implement event-driven programming through a GUI. You will also practice parsing XML or JSON files and representing that data in Java objects.

Step 1 Setting Up the Project Structure

Before diving into coding, let's break down the structure of the project. A well-organized project is essential for scalability and maintainability. The structure of our project will be as follows

Main Application Class This class will initialize the app and handle the overall flow of the program, such as loading questions and displaying the score at the end.

Question Class This will represent a single question in the quiz, including the question text, possible answers, and the correct answer.

Quiz Class This class will handle the quiz's logic, including keeping track of the user's answers and scoring.

FileParser Class This will parse the XML or JSON file to load the questions into the application.

User Interface (UI) The Swing components will be used for creating the user interface, which includes buttons, labels, and text fields for user interaction.

Step 2 Creating the Data Model (Question Class)

In any quiz app, questions are a central piece of the functionality. We need to represent each question in a way that is easy to manipulate within the app. The Question class will store all the information related to a single quiz question.

Here's a basic Question class

```
public class Question {
    private String questionText;
    private String[] options;
    private String correctAnswer;

    public Question(String questionText, String[]
options, String correctAnswer) {
        this.questionText = questionText;
        this.options = options;
        this.correctAnswer = correctAnswer;
    }

    public String getQuestionText() {
        return questionText;
    }

    public String[] getOptions() {
        return options;
```

```
    }

    public String getCorrectAnswer() {
        return correctAnswer;
    }

    public boolean isCorrect(String answer) {
        return this.correctAnswer.equals(answer);
    }
}
```

The `Question` class has the following attributes

questionText A string that contains the question itself.

options An array of strings representing the possible answers to the question.

correctAnswer A string representing the correct answer.

The constructor initializes these attributes, and the `isCorrect()` method checks whether a given answer is correct.

Step 3 Parsing Questions from a File (FileParser Class)

To load questions dynamically, we will store them in an external file in either XML or JSON format. Let's focus on JSON here, as it's a popular format for data interchange.

The `FileParser` class will handle reading the JSON file, parsing it, and converting the data into `Question` objects. We will use a simple JSON structure for storing the questions

```
[
  {
    "question"  "What is the capital of France?",
    "options"  ["Berlin", "Madrid", "Paris", "Rome"],
    "correctAnswer"  "Paris"
  },
  {
    "question"  "Which planet is known as the Red
Planet?",
    "options"  ["Earth", "Mars", "Jupiter",
"Saturn"],
    "correctAnswer"  "Mars"
  }
]
```

This JSON file represents a list of questions, where each object contains the question text, the answer options, and the correct answer.

Now, let's write the code to parse this JSON file

```
import org.json.JSONArray;
import org.json.JSONObject;

import java.io.File;
import java.io.FileReader;
import java.io.IOException;
import java.util.ArrayList;
import java.util.List;

public class FileParser {
```

```java
    public static List<Question>
parseQuestions(String filePath) {
        List<Question> questions = new ArrayList<>();
        try (FileReader reader = new FileReader(new
File(filePath))) {
            StringBuilder stringBuilder = new
StringBuilder();
            int i;
            while ((i = reader.read()) != -1) {
                stringBuilder.append((char) i);
            }

            JSONArray jsonQuestions = new
JSONArray(stringBuilder.toString());
            for (int j = 0; j <
jsonQuestions.length(); j++) {
                JSONObject jsonQuestion =
jsonQuestions.getJSONObject(j);
                String questionText =
jsonQuestion.getString("question");
                JSONArray jsonOptions =
jsonQuestion.getJSONArray("options");
                String[] options = new
String[jsonOptions.length()];
                for (int k = 0; k <
jsonOptions.length(); k++) {
                    options[k] =
jsonOptions.getString(k);
                }
                String correctAnswer =
jsonQuestion.getString("correctAnswer");

                Question question = new
Question(questionText, options, correctAnswer);
                questions.add(question);
            }

        } catch (IOException e) {
            e.printStackTrace();
        }
```

```
        return questions;
    }
}
```

In this code

- We use the `org.json` library to parse the JSON. Make sure to add the `json.jar` or `org.json` dependency to your project.
- We read the entire file into a `StringBuilder` and then parse the JSON into a `JSONArray`.
- For each question, we extract the question text, options, and correct answer, creating a new `Question` object and adding it to the list.

Step 4 Designing the User Interface (UI)

The user interface will be built using **Java Swing**, which is a rich GUI toolkit for building desktop applications. We will create a simple window displaying one question at a time, with radio buttons for the answer options and a submit button to check the answer.

Here's the basic layout for the UI

```
import javax.swing.*;
import java.awt.*;
import java.awt.event.ActionEvent;
import java.awt.event.ActionListener;

public class QuizApp extends JFrame {
    private int currentQuestionIndex = 0;
```

```java
    private int score = 0;
    private List<Question> questions;
    private JLabel questionLabel;
    private JRadioButton[] options;
    private ButtonGroup buttonGroup;

    public QuizApp(List<Question> questions) {
        this.questions = questions;
        setupUI();
    }

    private void setupUI() {
        setTitle("Java Quiz App");
        setSize(400, 300);

setDefaultCloseOperation(JFrame.EXIT_ON_CLOSE);
        setLayout(new BorderLayout());

        questionLabel = new JLabel("",
SwingConstants.CENTER);
        add(questionLabel, BorderLayout.NORTH);

        JPanel optionsPanel = new JPanel();
        optionsPanel.setLayout(new GridLayout(4, 1));
        options = new JRadioButton[4];
        buttonGroup = new ButtonGroup();
        for (int i = 0; i < 4; i++) {
            options[i] = new JRadioButton();
            buttonGroup.add(options[i]);
            optionsPanel.add(options[i]);
        }
        add(optionsPanel, BorderLayout.CENTER);

        JButton submitButton = new JButton("Submit");
        submitButton.addActionListener(new
SubmitButtonListener());
        add(submitButton, BorderLayout.SOUTH);

        showQuestion();
    }
```

```java
    private void showQuestion() {
        Question currentQuestion =
questions.get(currentQuestionIndex);

questionLabel.setText(currentQuestion.getQuestionText
());
        String[] optionsList =
currentQuestion.getOptions();
        for (int i = 0; i < optionsList.length; i++)
{
            options[i].setText(optionsList[i]);
        }
    }

    private class SubmitButtonListener implements
ActionListener {
        @Override
        public void actionPerformed(ActionEvent e) {
            Question currentQuestion =
questions.get(currentQuestionIndex);
            String selectedAnswer =
getSelectedAnswer();
            if
(currentQuestion.isCorrect(selectedAnswer)) {
                score++;
            }
            currentQuestionIndex++;
            if (currentQuestionIndex <
questions.size()) {
                showQuestion();
            } else {
                JOptionPane.showMessageDialog(null,
"Quiz Over! Your score  " + score);
                System.exit(0);
            }
        }
    }

    private String getSelectedAnswer() {
```

```java
        for (JRadioButton option   options) {
            if (option.isSelected()) {
                return option.getText();
            }
        }
        return "";
    }

    public static void main(String[] args) {
        List<Question> questions =
FileParser.parseQuestions("questions.json");
        QuizApp quizApp = new QuizApp(questions);
        quizApp.setVisible(true);
    }
}
```

In this `QuizApp` class

- We use `JLabel` to display the question text.
- `JRadioButton` components are used for the options. The `ButtonGroup` ensures that only one option can be selected at a time.

Chapter 15

Final Capstone Project – Multi-Tool Desktop Utility Suite

In this final chapter, we will consolidate everything you've learned so far by guiding you through the creation of a **Multi-Tool Java Desktop Utility Suite**. This project will combine several useful utilities into a single, cohesive application, and will teach you how to design a modular, extensible system where additional tools can be added easily via plugins or a menu system.

By the end of this project, you will have built a **desktop utility suite** that contains the following individual tools

1. **Task Manager**
2. **Notepad**
3. **Timer**
4. **File Cleaner**
5. **Password Vault**

These tools will provide a variety of functionalities, and the application will be designed in such a way that new tools can be added effortlessly.

This will not only challenge your skills in Java programming, but also give you hands-on experience in building a full-fledged desktop application. You will also gain knowledge in working with modularity, file handling, data security, and user interaction.

Setting Up the Project

Before we dive into the code, let's take a look at how we can structure the project for optimal maintainability and scalability. Since the goal is to build a **modular and extensible** system, the project should be organized in a way that allows easy addition of new tools.

The folder structure could look like this

```
MultiToolSuite/
│
├── src/
│     ├── TaskManager.java
│     ├── Notepad.java
│     ├── Timer.java
│     ├── FileCleaner.java
│     ├── PasswordVault.java
│     └── Main.java
│
├── Resources/
│     └── icons/           # Icons for each tool
(optional)
└── lib/                   # External libraries (if any)
```

This structure ensures that each tool is isolated in its own class, making it easy to add new tools in the future. Additionally, we'll also use a central `Main.java` class to initialize and manage all the tools.

Tool 1 Task Manager

A task manager allows the user to view and manage running processes on their system. For simplicity, we won't interact directly with the operating system's processes but will simulate a basic task manager that tracks tasks in a simple list.

Building the Task Manager

The core components of the Task Manager will include

List of Tasks This will display all tasks currently running.

Start Task A button to simulate starting a new task.

End Task A button to simulate terminating a task.

Here's a basic implementation of the `TaskManager` class

```
import javax.swing.*;
import java.awt.*;
import java.awt.event.ActionEvent;
import java.awt.event.ActionListener;
import java.util.ArrayList;

public class TaskManager extends JFrame {
    private DefaultListModel<String> taskListModel;
    private JList<String> taskList;
    private JButton startButton, endButton;

    public TaskManager() {
        setTitle("Task Manager");
        setSize(400, 300);
```

```java
setDefaultCloseOperation(JFrame.EXIT_ON_CLOSE);

        taskListModel = new DefaultListModel<>();
        taskList = new JList<>(taskListModel);
        JScrollPane scrollPane = new
JScrollPane(taskList);

        startButton = new JButton("Start Task");
        endButton = new JButton("End Task");

        startButton.addActionListener(new
StartTaskListener());
        endButton.addActionListener(new
EndTaskListener());

        setLayout(new BorderLayout());
        add(scrollPane, BorderLayout.CENTER);
        JPanel buttonPanel = new JPanel();
        buttonPanel.add(startButton);
        buttonPanel.add(endButton);
        add(buttonPanel, BorderLayout.SOUTH);
    }

    private class StartTaskListener implements
ActionListener {
        @Override
        public void actionPerformed(ActionEvent e) {
            String task = "Task " +
(taskListModel.getSize() + 1);
            taskListModel.addElement(task);
        }
    }

    private class EndTaskListener implements
ActionListener {
        @Override
        public void actionPerformed(ActionEvent e) {
            int selectedIndex =
taskList.getSelectedIndex();
```

```
                if (selectedIndex != -1) {
                    taskListModel.remove(selectedIndex);
                }
            }
        }

    public static void main(String[] args) {
        TaskManager taskManager = new TaskManager();
        taskManager.setVisible(true);
    }
}
```

In this code

- We use a `JList` to display the list of tasks.
- The **Start Task** button adds a new task to the list, while the **End Task** button removes a selected task from the list.

Tool 2 Notepad

The Notepad tool will provide a simple text editor where users can write and save notes. We will use a `JTextArea` for text input and a `JFileChooser` to allow the user to save and load files.

Building the Notepad

```
import javax.swing.*;
import java.awt.*;
import java.awt.event.*;
import java.io.*;

public class Notepad extends JFrame {
    private JTextArea textArea;
    private JMenuBar menuBar;
```

```java
    private JMenu fileMenu;
    private JMenuItem saveMenuItem, loadMenuItem;

    public Notepad() {
        setTitle("Notepad");
        setSize(500, 400);

setDefaultCloseOperation(JFrame.EXIT_ON_CLOSE);

        textArea = new JTextArea();
        JScrollPane scrollPane = new
JScrollPane(textArea);

        menuBar = new JMenuBar();
        fileMenu = new JMenu("File");
        saveMenuItem = new JMenuItem("Save");
        loadMenuItem = new JMenuItem("Open");

        saveMenuItem.addActionListener(new
SaveFileListener());
        loadMenuItem.addActionListener(new
LoadFileListener());

        fileMenu.add(saveMenuItem);
        fileMenu.add(loadMenuItem);
        menuBar.add(fileMenu);

        setJMenuBar(menuBar);
        add(scrollPane, BorderLayout.CENTER);
    }

    private class SaveFileListener implements
ActionListener {
        @Override
        public void actionPerformed(ActionEvent e) {
            JFileChooser fileChooser = new
JFileChooser();
            int result =
fileChooser.showSaveDialog(Notepad.this);
```

```java
                if (result ==
JFileChooser.APPROVE_OPTION) {
                    File file =
fileChooser.getSelectedFile();
                try (BufferedWriter writer = new
BufferedWriter(new FileWriter(file))) {
                    textArea.write(writer);
                } catch (IOException ex) {
                    ex.printStackTrace();
                }
            }
        }
    }

    private class LoadFileListener implements
ActionListener {
        @Override
        public void actionPerformed(ActionEvent e) {
            JFileChooser fileChooser = new
JFileChooser();
            int result =
fileChooser.showOpenDialog(Notepad.this);
            if (result ==
JFileChooser.APPROVE_OPTION) {
                File file =
fileChooser.getSelectedFile();
                try (BufferedReader reader = new
BufferedReader(new FileReader(file))) {
                    textArea.read(reader, null);
                } catch (IOException ex) {
                    ex.printStackTrace();
                }
            }
        }
    }

    public static void main(String[] args) {
        Notepad notepad = new Notepad();
        notepad.setVisible(true);
    }
```

```
}
```

The `Notepad` class provides basic functionality for saving and opening files. Users can interact with the text area, save their notes to a file, or load previous notes into the editor.

Tool 3 Timer

The Timer tool will provide a simple countdown timer. This could be useful for managing tasks, reminding the user to take breaks, or timing specific events.

Building the Timer

```
import javax.swing.*;
import java.awt.*;
import java.awt.event.*;
import java.util.Timer;
import java.util.TimerTask;

public class TimerTool extends JFrame {
    private JLabel timeLabel;
    private JButton startButton, stopButton;
    private Timer timer;
    private int timeLeft = 60;

    public TimerTool() {
        setTitle("Timer");
        setSize(200, 150);

setDefaultCloseOperation(JFrame.EXIT_ON_CLOSE);

        timeLabel = new JLabel("Time Left   " +
timeLeft, SwingConstants.CENTER);
        timeLabel.setFont(new Font("Serif",
Font.PLAIN, 20));
```

```java
        startButton = new JButton("Start");
        stopButton = new JButton("Stop");

        startButton.addActionListener(new
StartButtonListener());
        stopButton.addActionListener(new
StopButtonListener());

        setLayout(new BorderLayout());
        add(timeLabel, BorderLayout.CENTER);

        JPanel buttonPanel = new JPanel();
        buttonPanel.add(startButton);
        buttonPanel.add(stopButton);
        add(buttonPanel, BorderLayout.SOUTH);
    }

    private class StartButtonListener implements
ActionListener {
        @Override
        public void actionPerformed(ActionEvent e) {
            if (timer != null) {
                timer.cancel();
            }

            timer = new Timer();
            timer.scheduleAtFixedRate(new TimerTask()
{
                @Override
                public void run() {
                    timeLeft--;
                    timeLabel.setText("Time Left  " +
timeLeft);

                    if (timeLeft <= 0) {
                        timer.cancel();
                    }
                }
            }, 1000, 1000);
```

```
        }
    }

    private class StopButtonListener implements
ActionListener {
        @Override
        public void actionPerformed(ActionEvent e) {
            if (timer != null) {
                timer.cancel();
            }
            timeLeft = 60;
            timeLabel.setText("Time Left   " +
timeLeft);
        }
    }

    public static void main(String[] args) {
        TimerTool timerTool = new TimerTool();
        timerTool.setVisible(true);
    }
}
```

The **Timer** tool uses a `Timer` object and `TimerTask` to perform the countdown every second. The user can start and stop the timer with buttons.

Tool 4 File Cleaner

The **File Cleaner** tool will allow the user to clean up unnecessary files in a directory by removing them based on their size or extension. This could be used to remove temp files, logs, or other unwanted files.

Building the File Cleaner

```
import javax.swing.*;
import java.awt.*;
```

```java
import java.awt.event.*;
import java.io.*;
import java.nio.file.*;
import java.nio.file.attribute.*;

public class FileCleaner extends JFrame {
    private JButton cleanButton;

    public FileCleaner() {
        setTitle("File Cleaner");
        setSize(400, 200);

setDefaultCloseOperation(JFrame.EXIT_ON_CLOSE);

        cleanButton = new JButton("Clean Directory");

        cleanButton.addActionListener(new
CleanButtonListener());

        setLayout(new FlowLayout());
        add(cleanButton);
    }

    private class CleanButtonListener implements
ActionListener {
        @Override
        public void actionPerformed(ActionEvent e) {
            JFileChooser fileChooser = new
JFileChooser();

fileChooser.setFileSelectionMode(JFileChooser.DIRECTO
RIES_ONLY);
            int result =
fileChooser.showOpenDialog(FileCleaner.this);

            if (result ==
JFileChooser.APPROVE_OPTION) {
                File directory =
fileChooser.getSelectedFile();
                try {
```

```
                    Files.walk(directory.toPath())
                        .filter(path ->
path.toFile().isFile() && path.toFile().length() <
1024)
                            .forEach(path -> {
                                try {

Files.delete(path);
                                } catch (IOException
ex) {

ex.printStackTrace();
                                }
                            });

JOptionPane.showMessageDialog(null, "Files cleaned
up!");
                } catch (IOException ex) {
                    ex.printStackTrace();
                }
            }
        }
    }

    public static void main(String[] args) {
        FileCleaner fileCleaner = new FileCleaner();
        fileCleaner.setVisible(true);
    }
}
```

This code allows the user to select a directory, and it will clean files that are smaller than a specified size (e.g., 1KB). You can extend this tool to delete files based on other criteria.

Tool 5 Password Vault

A **Password Vault** securely stores and retrieves passwords for the user. In this implementation, we'll use simple encryption (e.g., AES) to store passwords securely.

Building the Password Vault

```java
import javax.swing.*;
import java.awt.*;
import java.awt.event.*;
import java.util.*;
import javax.crypto.*;
import javax.crypto.spec.*;
import java.util.Base64;

public class PasswordVault extends JFrame {
    private JTextField usernameField;
    private JPasswordField passwordField;
    private JButton saveButton, retrieveButton;
    private Map<String, String> passwordStore;

    public PasswordVault() {
        setTitle("Password Vault");
        setSize(400, 250);

setDefaultCloseOperation(JFrame.EXIT_ON_CLOSE);

        passwordStore = new HashMap<>();

        usernameField = new JTextField(20);
        passwordField = new JPasswordField(20);

        saveButton = new JButton("Save Password");
        retrieveButton = new JButton("Retrieve
Password");
```

```java
        saveButton.addActionListener(new
SavePasswordListener());
        retrieveButton.addActionListener(new
RetrievePasswordListener());

        setLayout(new FlowLayout());
        add(new JLabel("Username "));
        add(usernameField);
        add(new JLabel("Password "));
        add(passwordField);
        add(saveButton);
        add(retrieveButton);
    }

    private class SavePasswordListener implements
ActionListener {
        @Override
        public void actionPerformed(ActionEvent e) {
            String username =
usernameField.getText();
            String password = new
String(passwordField.getPassword());
            String encryptedPassword =
encryptPassword(password);
            passwordStore.put(username,
encryptedPassword);
        }
    }

    private class RetrievePasswordListener implements
ActionListener {
        @Override
        public void actionPerformed(ActionEvent e) {
            String username =
usernameField.getText();
            String encryptedPassword =
passwordStore.get(username);
            if (encryptedPassword != null) {
                String decryptedPassword =
decryptPassword(encryptedPassword);
```

```java
                    JOptionPane.showMessageDialog(null,
"Password  " + decryptedPassword);
            } else {
                JOptionPane.showMessageDialog(null,
"No password found for this username.");
            }
        }
    }


    private String encryptPassword(String password) {
        try {
            Cipher cipher =
Cipher.getInstance("AES");
            SecretKeySpec key = new
SecretKeySpec("1234567890123456".getBytes(), "AES");
            cipher.init(Cipher.ENCRYPT_MODE, key);
            byte[] encryptedBytes =
cipher.doFinal(password.getBytes());
            return
Base64.getEncoder().encodeToString(encryptedBytes);
        } catch (Exception ex) {
            ex.printStackTrace();
            return null;
        }
    }

    private String decryptPassword(String
encryptedPassword) {
        try {
            Cipher cipher =
Cipher.getInstance("AES");
            SecretKeySpec key = new
SecretKeySpec("1234567890123456".getBytes(), "AES");
            cipher.init(Cipher.DECRYPT_MODE, key);
            byte[] decryptedBytes =
cipher.doFinal(Base64.getDecoder().decode(encryptedPa
ssword));
            return new String(decryptedBytes);
        } catch (Exception ex) {
            ex.printStackTrace();
```

```
        return null;
    }
}

public static void main(String[] args) {
    PasswordVault passwordVault = new
PasswordVault();
    passwordVault.setVisible(true);
    }
}
```

This class allows the user to store passwords securely. The passwords are encrypted using **AES** encryption before they are saved and decrypted when they are retrieved.

Integrating the Tools into the Main Suite

Once all the tools are created, the final step is to integrate them into the main application. The Main.java class will serve as the entry point to the suite. You'll need to create a menu or plugin system that allows the user to choose which tool they want to use.

In this setup, you can either create a **menu system** where each tool is listed as an item in a dropdown menu, or you could use a **plugin-based** system where new tools are dynamically added to the application at runtime. For the sake of simplicity, let's use a menu system that loads each tool in a new window.

By completing this **Multi-Tool Desktop Utility Suite**, you will have learned how to

- Build a **modular** system where new tools can be added easily.
- Handle various user interfaces using **Swing**.
- Implement **file handling**, **encryption**, and other essential desktop application techniques.
- Develop a **full-featured** application that brings together multiple practical tools.

This final project will serve as a **capstone** to your journey, helping you reinforce your understanding of Java and desktop application development while giving you a tangible product to showcase.

Chapter 16

Packaging and Distributing Java Desktop Apps

In this chapter, we will explore the process of **packaging** and **distributing** Java desktop applications. We will teach you how to take your completed Java project and prepare it for release, ensuring that it is easy for others to install and use. This process will include converting your Java application into **JAR (Java ARchive)** files, and we will also cover the creation of **native installers** for different operating systems. Additionally, we will discuss **version control** using **Git**, techniques for **code refactoring**, and how to create proper **documentation** for your project.

The goal of this chapter is not only to ensure that your Java desktop app can be distributed but also to provide you with the tools and techniques needed to maintain and improve your application over time. Whether you plan to distribute your app to colleagues, friends, or a larger audience, this chapter will guide you through the essential steps.

Packaging Java Applications as JAR Files

Java applications are often distributed in the form of **JAR files**. A **JAR file** is essentially a compressed archive that contains all the classes and resources of your application, making it easy to distribute and run.

Step 1 Preparing Your Project for Packaging

Before creating a JAR file, you need to make sure that your project is in a **clean state**. This means ensuring that all your source code is compiled, and any unnecessary files are removed. Here's what you should do

Ensure all dependencies are in place If your project uses external libraries, make sure they are included in the project.

Organize the files Place all your `.class` files, resources (such as images or sounds), and configuration files into appropriate directories.

Step 2 Creating a JAR File

To package your application into a JAR file, you can use the **Java Development Kit (JDK)**. The `jar` tool comes bundled with the JDK and allows you to package your files into a `.jar` archive.

Here's a simple way to create a JAR file from the command line

1. Navigate to the root directory of your project.
2. Use the `jar` command to package your classes and resources into a JAR file.

For example, if your project has a directory structure like this

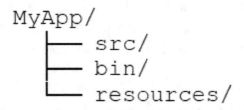

You can create a JAR file by running the following command

```
jar cvf MyApp.jar -C bin/ .
```

In this command

- `cvf` tells the JAR tool to **create** a new archive, **verbose** (show the process), and **file** (output the archive to a file).
- `MyApp.jar` is the name of the output JAR file.
- `-C bin/` specifies the directory where the compiled `.class` files are stored.
- The `.` indicates that all files in the `bin/` directory should be added to the JAR file.

The result will be a JAR file that you can distribute.

Step 3 Running the JAR File

Once your JAR file is created, you can run it from the command line using the following command

```
java -jar MyApp.jar
```

This assumes that the `Main` class in your project contains a `public static void main(String[] args)` method. If your main class has a different name, you will need to specify it when creating the JAR file using a manifest.

Creating Native Installers with `jpackage`, Inno Setup

While JAR files are a great way to distribute Java applications, some users may prefer to install your app like any other desktop application. This is where **native installers** come in. Native installers allow your Java app to be installed on Windows, macOS, or Linux just like other native applications, providing a more seamless experience for the end user.

Using `jpackage` to Create Native Installers

Java 14 introduced the `jpackage` tool, which allows you to create native installers for Windows, macOS, and Linux. With `jpackage`, you can package your JAR file into a native executable that can be run without needing the user to have Java installed.

Here's a basic example of how to create a native installer using `jpackage`

1. First, compile your application and generate a JAR file.
2. Run `jpackage` with the following command

```
jpackage --input ./bin --name MyApp --main-jar
MyApp.jar --main-class com.myapp.Main --type dmg
```

In this command

- `--input ./bin` specifies the directory where your compiled `.jar` file is located.
- `--name MyApp` sets the name of your application.
- `--main-jar MyApp.jar` specifies the main JAR file to run.
- `--main-class com.myapp.Main` specifies the fully-qualified name of your main class.
- `--type dmg` specifies the type of installer to create (you can also choose `msi` for Windows, or `deb` for Linux).

`jpackage` will generate a native installer based on the selected platform.

Using Inno Setup for Windows Installers

If you are targeting **Windows**, **Inno Setup** is a popular tool for creating professional-looking installers. With Inno Setup, you can bundle your JAR file and all its dependencies into an executable installer.

Here's how you can create an installer using Inno Setup

1. Download and install **Inno Setup** from here.
2. Create an Inno Setup script (.iss file) that defines how your application will be installed. A simple script might look like this

```
[Setup]
AppName=MyApp
AppVersion=1.0
DefaultDirName={pf}\MyApp
DefaultGroupName=MyApp
OutputDir=.\Output
OutputBaseFilename=MyAppInstaller

[Files]
Source  "C \path\to\MyApp.jar"; DestDir  "{app}";
Flags  ignoreversion
Source  "C \path\to\java\bin\java.exe"; DestDir
"{app}"; Flags  ignoreversion

[Run]
Filename  "{app}\java.exe"; Parameters  "-jar
MyApp.jar"; WorkingDir  "{app}"; Flags  nowait
postinstall
```

3. Compile the `.iss` file using the Inno Setup compiler, which will generate an `.exe` installer.

Using Launch4j for Windows Executables

If you want to create a Windows **EXE** file from your Java application, **Launch4j** is an excellent tool that wraps a JAR file into a native executable.

To use Launch4j

1. Download and install **Launch4j** from here.
2. Open Launch4j and configure the following
   - **Input file** Your JAR file.
   - **Output file** The location of the generated EXE file.
   - **JRE path** The path to the JRE on the user's machine (if you want to bundle the JRE).

Once configured, Launch4j will generate a Windows executable that runs your JAR file.

Version Control Using Git

Version control is an essential part of any software development process. Git is the most widely used version control system and allows you to track changes to your code, collaborate with other developers, and maintain a history of your project.

To get started with Git

Initialize a Git repository In your project directory, run the following command to initialize a Git repository

```
git init
```

Add your project files Add all the project files to the staging area

```
git add .
```

Commit your changes Commit the added files with a descriptive message

```
git commit -m "Initial commit of the Java desktop app"
```

Create a remote repository Create a new repository on a platform like **GitHub**, **GitLab**, or **Bitbucket**. Then link your local repository to the remote one

```
git remote add origin <repository_url>
```

Push your changes Push your code to the remote repository

```
git push -u origin master
```

By using Git, you ensure that you can keep track of changes, collaborate with others, and have a backup of your code.

Code Refactoring Techniques

As your project grows, it's essential to **refactor** your code to maintain clarity, reduce redundancy, and improve maintainability. Here are some key refactoring techniques

Extract Methods If you find yourself repeating code, consider creating a method that can be reused.

Simplify Complex Conditionals If you have complicated conditional logic, break it into smaller, more understandable parts.

Encapsulate Fields Use **getter** and **setter** methods to provide controlled access to fields, instead of allowing direct access.

Use Meaningful Names Choose descriptive names for variables, methods, and classes to make your code easier to understand.

Refactoring doesn't mean adding new features; rather, it's about cleaning up and improving the existing code to make it easier to work with and extend in the future.

Documenting Your Application

Finally, **documentation** is crucial for both users and developers. Proper documentation helps users understand how to use the application, and it helps other developers (or your future self) understand how the code works and how it can be extended or modified.

Your documentation should include

README File A simple text or markdown file that explains what the application does, how to install it, and how to use it.

Code Comments Inside your code, use comments to explain complex logic, clarify the purpose of functions, and document any important sections of code.

Appendices

The following appendices provide valuable additional resources to help you deepen your knowledge and improve your skills as you build Java-based desktop applications. Whether you're looking to expand your toolkit with new libraries, troubleshoot common issues, or plan your future learning path, this section will guide you toward further mastery.

Appendix A

Java Swing Component Reference

Java Swing is a popular GUI framework used to build desktop applications. It provides a rich set of **graphical components** that allow developers to create user interfaces that are both functional and visually appealing. The following is a comprehensive reference guide to some of the most commonly used **Swing components**.

JFrame

The JFrame class is the most basic container for a GUI. It represents a top-level window with a title, border, and buttons for closing, minimizing, and maximizing. Typically, this is the main window that houses all other components.

Example

```
JFrame frame = new JFrame("My Application");
frame.setSize(400, 300);
frame.setDefaultCloseOperation(JFrame.EXIT_ON_CLOSE);
frame.setVisible(true);
```

JPanel

JPanel is a generic container used to hold other Swing components. It's often used to organize components within the JFrame.

Example

```
JPanel panel = new JPanel();
panel.setLayout(new FlowLayout());
panel.add(new JLabel("Enter your name "));
panel.add(new JTextField(20));
```

```
frame.add(panel);
```

JButton

JButton is used to create a clickable button. Buttons can be used to trigger actions in your application.

Example

```
JButton button = new JButton("Click Me!");
button.addActionListener(new ActionListener() {
        public void actionPerformed(ActionEvent e) {
        System.out.println("Button was clicked!");
        }
});
```

JTextField

JTextField is used to create a single-line text input field. It allows users to enter text.

Example

```
JTextField textField = new JTextField(20);
panel.add(textField);
```

JTextArea

JTextArea is a multi-line text input field. It can be used to display long text or allow users to enter several lines of input.

Example

```
JTextArea textArea = new JTextArea(10, 30);
textArea.setText("Initial text");
panel.add(new JScrollPane(textArea)); // Adding
scroll functionality
```

JLabel

`JLabel` is used to display a short piece of text or an image. It cannot be edited by the user.

Example

```
JLabel label = new JLabel("Username ");
panel.add(label);
```

JComboBox

`JComboBox` creates a drop-down list of options from which the user can choose.

Example

```
String[] options = { "Option 1", "Option 2", "Option
3" };
JComboBox<String> comboBox = new
JComboBox<>(options);
panel.add(comboBox);
```

Appendix B

JDBC Cheat Sheet for SQLite & MySQL

Java Database Connectivity (JDBC) allows you to interact with databases from Java. Whether you're using **SQLite** for local applications or **MySQL** for web-connected systems, JDBC provides a standard API for database interactions. Below is a cheat sheet to quickly recall common operations when working with **SQLite** and **MySQL** databases.

1. Establishing a Connection

- **SQLite**

```
Connection conn =
DriverManager.getConnection("jdbc sqlite
path_to_db");
```

- **MySQL**

```
Connection conn =
DriverManager.getConnection("jdbc mysql
//localhost 3306/mydb", "username",
"password");
```

2. Creating a Statement

- **SQLite**

```
Statement stmt = conn.createStatement();
```

- **MySQL**

```
Statement stmt = conn.createStatement();
```

3. Executing SQL Queries

- **SQLite** (SELECT query)
  ```
  ResultSet rs = stmt.executeQuery("SELECT * FROM
  users");
  while (rs.next()) {

  System.out.println(rs.getString("username"));
  }
  ```

- **MySQL** (INSERT query)
  ```
  tring query = "INSERT INTO users (username,
  password) VALUES ('john', 'password123')";
  stmt.executeUpdate(query);
  ```

4. PreparedStatement for Parameterized Queries

- **SQLite**

  ```
  String sql = "INSERT INTO users (username,
  password) VALUES (?, ?)";
  PreparedStatement pstmt =
  conn.prepareStatement(sql);
  pstmt.setString(1, "john");
  pstmt.setString(2, "password123");
  pstmt.executeUpdate();
  ```

- **MySQL**

  ```
  String sql = "INSERT INTO users (username,
  password) VALUES (?, ?)";
  PreparedStatement pstmt =
  conn.prepareStatement(sql);
  pstmt.setString(1, "john");
  pstmt.setString(2, "password123");
  pstmt.executeUpdate();
  ```

Appendix C

Libraries & Frameworks for Java GUI Development

There are several libraries and frameworks available that can enhance your Java GUI applications. These libraries provide additional functionality, support for newer UI paradigms, and help streamline development.

JavaFX

JavaFX is an advanced framework for building modern, rich user interfaces in Java. It provides a wide range of features, including 2D/3D graphics, media playback, and web content embedding. Although Swing is more widely used in legacy applications, JavaFX is more suited for newer, visually rich applications.

JFreeChart

JFreeChart is a popular library for creating charts and graphs in Java applications. It can be used to create pie charts, bar charts, line charts, and more, making it a great tool for displaying dynamic data in your application.

JCommon

JCommon is a general-purpose library often used alongside JFreeChart for common utilities and support classes.

Apache POI

Apache POI is a powerful library for reading and writing Microsoft Office file formats (e.g., Excel, Word). If your application needs to handle office documents, Apache POI is a must-have.

Gson

Gson is a library for converting Java objects to JSON and vice versa. It's very helpful when you need to store or exchange data in JSON format.

Log4j

Log4j is a logging utility that helps in tracking the flow of an application. It allows you to record various levels of logs, such as `info`, `warn`, and `error`, which are invaluable for debugging and monitoring applications.

Appendix D

Troubleshooting & Debugging Common Errors

As you develop Java desktop applications, you will encounter errors and bugs that need to be addressed. The ability to troubleshoot and debug effectively is crucial for any developer. This appendix covers common issues and solutions.

Common Issues in Java GUI Development

NullPointerException

This error occurs when your code tries to access an object or method from a `null` reference. Ensure that all objects are properly instantiated before usage.

Solution Check for null references before using them.

```
if (myObject != null) {
        myObject.someMethod();
}
```

UI Freezing

Swing applications often freeze if the **Event Dispatch Thread (EDT)** is blocked by long-running tasks. This can occur if you perform time-consuming operations on the main thread.

Solution Use `SwingWorker` to execute long tasks in the background.

```
SwingWorker<Void, Void> worker = new
SwingWorker<Void, Void>() {
        @Override
        protected Void doInBackground() throws
        Exception {
```

```
        // Long-running task
        return null;
        }
        @Override
        protected void done() {
        // Update UI after task is done
        }
};
        worker.execute();
```

Component Not Showing on Screen

If your Swing components aren't showing, it could be due to an issue with layout management or missing calls to `revalidate()` or `repaint()`.

Solution Ensure your frame and panels are properly added and validated.

```
frame.add(panel);
frame.revalidate();
frame.repaint();
```

Appendix E

Future Learning Paths – JavaFX, Spring Boot

As you gain more experience with Java development, you may want to explore additional technologies and frameworks that can expand your capabilities and career opportunities. The following are some potential future learning paths.

JavaFX for Rich Desktop UIs

JavaFX is the successor to Swing and provides a more modern approach to building graphical user interfaces. It supports advanced features like 2D/3D graphics, animations, and media handling. JavaFX is highly recommended for developers who want to create visually rich applications with a modern feel.

Spring Boot for Backend Development

While JavaFX and Swing are geared towards **front-end** desktop development, **Spring Boot** is a popular framework for building Java-based **back-end** services. Spring Boot simplifies the process of developing web applications, REST APIs, and microservices. If you're interested in full-stack development, learning Spring Boot would be a great next step.

Mobile App Development with Java

If you're interested in developing mobile applications, Java is still widely used in **Android development** through the **Android SDK**. You can learn how to create mobile apps with Java by diving into Android development, which offers vast opportunities in the mobile app market.

By mastering these frameworks and learning new technologies, you'll enhance your development skills and be able to take on more complex projects in Java. Each learning path opens up exciting possibilities, whether you choose to develop powerful desktop apps, back-end services, or mobile apps.

THE END

www.ingramcontent.com/pod-product-compliance
Lightning Source LLC
La Vergne TN
LVHW051330050326
832903LV00031B/3456